The Carbon Efficient City

A-P HURD + AL HURD

Foreword by Denis Hayes

THE CARBON EFFICIENT CITY

UNIVERSITY OF WASHINGTON PRESS *Seattle & London*

© 2012 BY THE UNIVERSITY OF WASHINGTON PRESS
16 15 14 13 12   5 4 3 2 1

University of Washington Press
PO Box 50096, Seattle, WA 98145, USA
www.washington.edu/uwpress

LIBRARY OF CONGRESS CATALOGING-IN-PUBLICATION DATA
Hurd, A-P.
The carbon efficient city / A-P Hurd and Al Hurd ; foreword by Denis Hayes.
p. cm.
Includes bibliographical references and index.
ISBN 978-0-295-99171-9 (pbk : alk. paper)
1. Sustainable urban development. 2. Carbon dioxide mitigation. 3. Urban ecology (Sociology) 4. City planning—Environmental aspects. I. Hurd, Al. II. Title.
HT241.H87 2012
363.738'746—dc23   2012003862

Printed and bound in the United States of America
Designed by Ashley Saleeba
Composed in Fanwood by Barry Schwartz, courtesy The League of Movable Type
Display type set in Univers by Adrian Frutiger, courtesy Adobe Systems

The paper used in this publication is acid-free and meets the minimum requirements of American National Standard for Information Sciences—Permanence of Paper for Printed Library Materials, ANSI Z39.48–1984.∞

To Marie-Andrée, who instilled in me a fundamental impatience to fix things that are wrong, and to Josh and Em, who remind me to laugh at these same things—and at myself—when I come home.

—A-P HURD

To Sue, whose patience and unconditional support make it possible for me to dive into missions that excite me, like this book.

—AL HURD

CONTENTS

Foreword / BY DENIS HAYES

Cities and city living are a modern development. For the first 200,000 years of human history, people were hunter-gatherers, living in small groups and moving frequently. The development of agriculture some 10,000 years ago allowed people to establish the first permanent settlements in the form of small villages with tiny populations.

The first true city to emerge was Uruk, the capital of Sumeria, in the southern part of what is now Iraq. By 5,000 years ago Uruk had at least 50,000 inhabitants, but the city and the entire Sumerian civilization eventually disappeared as a result of environmentally damaging agricultural practices. Without effective management, the very thing that made large settlements possible—an agricultural system that produced sufficient surpluses to support urban life—destroyed long-term sustainability.

After Uruk, cities came and went—Rome, Byzantium, Xi'an, Rajasthan, Alexandria—but widespread urbanization of the population is a relatively new phenomenon. As recently as two hundred years ago, only 3 percent of the world's people lived in cities. By one hundred years ago, the number of urbanites had grown to just 12 percent.

When I was born, about 500 million of the world's 2.3 billion people lived in cities. Today, in 2012, urban dwellers number about 3.5 billion. If I outlive my actuarial life expectancy (I'd like to shoot for ninety years), when I die these numbers will have grown to 5.5 billion people living in cities, out of a total world population of more than 8 billion. During my lifetime alone, then, the world's cities will have acquired approximately 5 billion people. Is it any wonder most cities are dysfunctional?

Cities keep getting bigger and bigger. Today, the world has about four hundred cities with more than one million inhabitants each. Forty have more than 5 million; nineteen have more than 10 million. Many of these are essentially congested chaos—but not because we don't know how to design livable cities. Many urban settings are healthy, convenient, prosperous, stimulating, safe, sustainable places to live and work. I'm thinking of cities like Reykjavik, Vancouver, B.C., Malmo, Copenhagen, Curitiba, and Portland, Oregon.

We have deep knowledge about how to build cities that are carbon efficient. We know that cities can find solutions to global problems such as climate change, rather than creating greater energy and livability problems because of their sheer size. The problem, as I see it, is that we cannot organize sufficient political will, amid the explosive growth, to implement the policies that produce coherent and sustainable urban design.

We know what to do; we just don't know how to persuade or cajole or require ourselves to do it. That is the problem that A-P Hurd and Al Hurd set out to address.

The Carbon Efficient City recognizes that our species is making an unprecedented evolutionary leap—within a single lifespan—from a predominantly rural population to one that is overwhelmingly urban. We are feeling our way forward and will inevitably make mistakes in planning and managing the population shift. The Hurds are refreshingly candid about the magnitude of the effort needed and the constraints imposed by the current political landscape. Yet they remain hopeful.

Whether or not one accepts all of the book's assumptions or agrees with all of its recommendations, most readers will find the suggestions here thoughtful and provocative— and this makes me hopeful. Only by tackling the tough questions and thinking systemically can we get where we need to go.

This is pressing work. Read on.

Preface

The idea for this book came out of the Quality Growth Alliance, a Puget Sound organization that brought together a diverse group of business, urban, and environmental interests who agreed on how growth should be accommodated in the region. In 2009, I was part of the alliance's initial working group on carbon emissions and was looking for a comprehensive resource that addressed the built environment's impact on carbon emissions. At the time there were many new (and not-so-new) strategies being embraced in building design and an emerging interest in the role of land use and transportation as part of the solution to climate change. Existing works tended to focus on specific technologies (green roofs, solar energy, walkable streets), but none provided a good survey across all the necessary strategies to consider in concert with each other. Even those works that grouped certain strategies together in one book tended to focus either on the building or on the urban environment.

With some encouragement from the working group, I began to pursue the idea of a compendium and to look for an expert who might have the time and wherewithal to put such a document together. Several conversations and grant applications later, it occurred to me that it might be more productive to just take a crack at this project myself. Over the summer of 2009, I worked on an outline for "the handbook," trying to distill built environment energy strategies into eight to ten manageable buckets. From my experience in building design and real estate development, I knew that many of these strategies were technically sound but challenging to implement in practice. As I worked on the handbook, it evolved from a list into a matrix, where the strategies were cross-referenced with the institutions that impact building and urban development: municipal governments, investors, and state governments. It was hard to think about what needed to be done in technical terms alone; I quickly realized that this project needed to address the legal and economic frameworks we operate in, just as much as the technical strategies.

The project had grown from a handbook into something more like a real book. By the fall of 2009, I knew I couldn't research, write, and edit the whole project myself. My dad, Al Hurd, had just retired from a career as an executive in the information technology industry, and I asked him if he would work on the project with me if I went ahead with turning the six-thousand-word outline into a full draft. Neither of us knew at the time that this would become a two-year intellectual collaboration that has been incredibly rewarding for both us. Relatively few people have the opportunity to engage in this type of partnership with their parent. To be able to work with someone who understands you so well, with whom you have such a high degree of trust, who may have a different style but who shares a similar sensibility is a gift. My father and I found that we appreciated each other's judgment, edits, and ideas. Our debates were productive and satisfyingly resolved. It has been a pleasure to work together in this way.

The resulting book is fundamentally a pragmatic one. We are passionate about slowing climate change but recognize at a deep level that our development patterns, cities, and buildings are shaped by economics. Those who see regulation as a stand-alone solution must recognize that regulation has its limits in a capitalist democracy. If our economic and political institutions are a given, how much change can we accomplish within these very real constraints? After a couple of years of pushing on these ideas, I'm happy to say that the answer may be "quite a lot" and possibly even "enough."

Some readers of the original manuscript recommended that the book also address the politics of suggested practices. While there is no doubt that political strategy is required to implement any idea, and this book has economic, legal and policy ideas, a "political" book in an age of partisan politics can be the death knell of good ideas. The concepts presented here are worth embracing because they are economically sound and supported by a strong, transparent, and efficient economic system. Furthermore, politics is local. One person may embrace public transit because it's "green," the next may see its value in fostering greater energy independence as a key component of national security, while still another may see it as a way to move more people on existing infrastructure and keep taxes low. Politicians, nonprofits, industry associations, and citizen advocates need to find the political levers that resonate most with their representatives and constituents and with their own truth.

There is still so much work to be done, and in such a short time. I hope that others engaged in similar efforts find this book to be a useful resource, one that they can build on with other ideas, insights, and strategies.

A-P HURD
Seattle

Acknowledgments

This book has been supported by a broad community of ideas in Seattle and across the country. In every way it defies the narrative of the lone hero engaged in a magnum opus in some faraway garret.

First, in its genesis, we thank the Quality Growth Alliance and Forterra (the organization formerly known as Cascade Land Conservancy) for their groundbreaking work in bringing business and environmental interests into such a mutually productive conversation. This book would not have been written without the discourse and sense of possibility created by these two organizations.

Second, in practical matters, we owe great thanks to the Runstad Center for Real Estate and the College of Built Environments at the University of Washington. A-P has been an affiliate fellow of the college since 2009 and has benefited from innumerable conversations and exchanges with students and faculty alike. The college and Dean Daniel Friedman generously provided a quiet space to write the first draft, support for the ideas, and encouragement to publish the work. Perhaps most important, by renaming the College of Built Environments, Dean Friedman has brought about a profound recognition in the academic community that we are engaged in a fundamentally interdisciplinary field with broad impacts and great responsibilities. George Rolfe, the co-director of the Runstad Center, has been a tireless supporter of this project and of A-P's other wild ideas. Thank you, George, for your confidence, your perspective, and your vision.

Among other gifts, the college introduced us to Julia Levitt and generously funded a research assistant position that brought resources to our work. That sentence makes it sound a little like all resources are created equal, and Julia is most certainly not. Julia Levitt brought ideas, patience, good humor, rigorous execution, and a helpful perspective. We would have been hard pressed to navigate the publication process without her advice. She is a gem. Someday she will be famous and we will tell people we knew her back when.

Douglas Howe at Touchstone generously provided a few much-needed "vacation days" to write a first draft back when this was a glimmer in A-P's eye. Glenn Amster also believed in this project from that first lunch at the Daily Grill and provided a great deal of early input on the outline and drafts. Rich Hill—good judgment is only a phone call away—made several helpful suggestions on the outline, including an admonishment against wishful thinking that became a bit of a mantra for our team. Susan Drummond was perhaps the earliest enthusiast for this project and has been steadfast in her support and collaboration on other related work. In San Francisco, Rachel Sheinbein, doing her own clean tech work, has been an ongoing sounding board, cheerleader, reviewer, and true believer.

The professional and built environment community has supported this book in so many ways: Gene Duvernoy, Bill Ruckelshaus, Denis Hayes, Denis Wilde, Bill Reed, Carol Sanford, and Ed Mazria have all provided perspective and encouragement. With godfathers like this believing in the project, it was easy for us to keep going. Rachel Cardone provided early insights and encouragement, and made an invaluable introduction to Cristina Rumbaitis Del Rio at the Rockefeller Foundation, whom we never met in person but who was so generous with telephone conversations, contacts, and resources, that we came to think of her as a fairy godmother. Jason McLennan provided early insight into the world of publishing, and we referenced the notes from that conversation again and again. Tamar Haspel continued to fill in that roadmap as we went along. Jason Twill tapped his remarkable network to help us find primary sources for many of our stories. Kelly Mann at ULI Seattle, Suzanne Cartwright, Kate Knight, Rae Anne Rushing, Patrick Mazza of Climate Solutions, Tom Bisacquino at NAIOP National, and A-P's NAIOP Forum members all provided encouragement and advice that kept us on the right track. Finally, Tim Mennel, Uwe Brandes, and Jeevan Sivasubramaniam all went far beyond the call of duty to provide thoughtful strategic advice about how to get the book into print.

Lorri Hagman at University of Washington Press understood the book from the first time we spoke and was willing to take a chance on us. We are immensely grateful for her faith in us and for all the editorial and technical help from the team at the University of Washington Press. Liz Dunn, whom we later found out had peer-reviewed the book, took a huge part of her Christmas vacation to provide excellent and detailed insight on the content, including steering us to the ideas of Donella Meadows and Gerald Frug, whose work in turn strengthened our analysis.

Finally, this book would not have been possible without our friends and extended family. Rob Spooner made the clean communicative graphics. Soren Eberhardt helped navigate the German bureaucracy on a moment's notice. Richard Austin provided no small measure of legal perspective, common sense, and a non-built-environment lens. Doug Barkley, an avid reader of business books, gave us his seasoned and typically frank advice on how to get the introduction right. Josh Binder has fed A-P's brain with dinnertime economics and generally kept the "systems thinking" alive on the home front. Keir Dahlke helped with photos, with the Web site, and even dug up an old cell phone on eBay so we could get a picture of it. Skene Howie pinch-hit on a missing photo. And, last but not least, Sue Wilson contributed countless hours to this project reviewing manuscripts, building the Web site, vetting ideas, and generally embracing the work that has consumed so much of Al's "retirement." Sue, we could not be where we are without you.

The Carbon Efficient City

INTRODUCTION

The most striking thing about climate change is that despite the best efforts of so many people, our planet's inhabitants seem incapable of doing anything about it. Although some uncertainty remains about the significance of humans' role in climate change, there is no longer any doubt that CO_2 molecules in the atmosphere increase the earth's retention of the sun's heat. There is no question either that over the past two hundred years of industrialization, human output of CO_2 into the atmosphere has relentlessly increased.[1]

No one can tell how our climate will change in the next fifty to two hundred years. All the incredibly complex models produced by climatologists are just that—models. When all is said and done, they give us a distribution of possible climate outcomes—some of which could simply be a challenge to live with and deprive of us of polar bears, and others which could entail staggering economic and social costs and ultimately change patterns of human life on earth. Predicting long-range climate trends is a probabilistic science, and some outcomes are more likely than others, but there is a good chance that we will face significant impacts to our quality of life in the next fifty to one hundred years—indeed, many who have lived through the increasingly frequent climate events of the past few decades, such as unusually intense hurricanes in the United States or prolonged severe droughts followed by unprecedented flooding in Australia, would argue that we already have.[2]

Since the early 2000s, as awareness of climate change has increased, our society has mobilized in important but fragmented ways to lower our CO_2 output. Automobile companies are focusing considerable effort on fuel efficiency and on developing alternative fuel vehicles at the same time as they continue to satisfy market demand for large numbers of SUVs. Former presidents and vice presidents have provided considerable leadership on climate issues while those in office have been more cautious. Universities around the world have made it their focus, but industrial standards have lagged. Think tanks have sprung up or reoriented around the challenge of climate change. And what have we to show for this? Not a 50 percent drop in emissions in exchange for our 50 percent focus, but only a slight flattening in an upward trajectory that may be caused as much by the global economic slowdown of 2008 to 2011 as by any of these efforts.[3] We have a lot of people pushing in the right direction, but the output of the system as a whole is not changing very much at all. To understand why, it will help if we make a brief detour into the science of how systems work.

A Systems Problem

Both climate change and the solution to it are systems challenges. Our planet is a system that is regulated and stabilized by a series of physical and biological feedback loops that exist at large and small scales and that are influenced by all the participants in the system. The solution to climate change is dependent on the planet's physical system and on the political and regulatory forces that themselves constitute a related social system. Now for some of the basics of systems theory:

» Because there are so many interrelated forces in a system, changing a few ingredients often doesn't have a big impact on the outcome. This is actually a positive feature of systems in many instances and is known as *resilience*. Resilience is what allows people around the world to eat all sorts of different foods and still express their DNA in essentially the same way.

» This inherent tendency of a system to maintain a balanced equilibrium (referred to as its steady state) also means that if it headed toward an undesirable outcome, it could be pretty hard to get things going in a better direction. If we think about how fossil fuels have become so integral to our society, we begin to realize that emitting carbon has become part

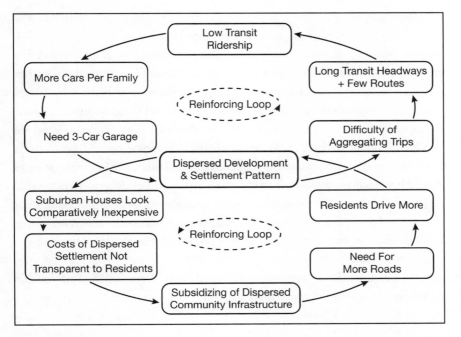

I.1
Example of two
reinforcing system
loops for dispersed
settlemenst patterns

of our system's current steady state. That makes it a considerable challenge to figure out how to change our outputs.

» However, when the forces in a system become too strong to be balanced by the rest of the system, equilibrium is overcome and the system is headed for a (possibly fundamentally) different state.

Figure I.1 provides an illustration of how a system can become stabilized in a particular pattern of behavior. In the example we can see how a disbursed settlement pattern leads to weak public transit and a consequent need for more private cars and more roads, all of which reinforce disbursed settlement. Once the system settles into this state, it becomes very hard to break out of the loop.

In the 2008 book *Thinking in Systems,* Donella Meadows, the renowned system theorist from MIT, addresses how to effect change by suggesting that there are twelve points of leverage that can be used to alter the course of a system.[4] Meadows's first three leverage points are related to goals and paradigms of the system. The next nine deal with the mechanics of how the system works and include metrics, feedback loops, information flows, and rules. Understanding these two types of leverage points is critical to making progress and mitigating climate change.

Changing Climate System Goals

Unquestionably, the data from climate scientists have begun to impact our system goals. Despite the ebb and flow of public opinion, there are very few other problems that have galvanized so much of society across so many institutions. Getting to the moon was essentially the effort of one government. Giving women the vote was a shaking of the political tree. The combustion engine was a product of industry. Our efforts related to climate change, by contrast, have sprung from nearly every institution and sector of society. Yet for many people the goal of reducing carbon emissions is still a "nice to have"—not a "need." It's not quite at the level of surpassing other priorities, like a quick trip to work, a face-to-face client meeting across the country, or a winter box of blueberries flown in from Chile. Why is it so hard to make climate stability a high-priority system goal?

We are a society that pays homage to data; at the same time we are biologically wired to attribute a higher likelihood to events for which we have powerful anecdotes. Many people are fearful of visiting Israel because of the perceived threat of political violence, which they hear about in the news; from an analytical perspective a visitor to Israel is much more likely to die in a car accident. Similarly, many people today believe that it is less safe than it used to be to let small children run around the neighborhood unsupervised; they are nostalgic for the relative security of their own childhoods. In actuality, however, crime has dropped in nearly every major American city since the 1970s. It is the *stories* of crimes—particularly those against children that are widely reported—that create a perception of increased danger.

Why is this important? Because climate change is an inherently abstract concept, there are few anecdotal or human interest stories on television that are tied directly to its impact. The absence of these stories makes it difficult to mobilize voters around the urgency of the issue. In addition, the long-term nature of the problem makes it even less of a good news story. People love watching car chases on the evening news; they are significantly less interested in data that have consequences outside their lifetimes. It is the difficulty of substantially impacting the system goal, of creating a strong link between data and human impact, that has been responsible for some of the recent failures to change energy and emissions legislation. If we are honest, we need to acknowledge that it will take time to build up the human stories that can give people a gut feeling for the consequences of climate change that can move them to action. Despite the setbacks, however, there a few good reasons to believe that climate stability will become a more prominent and prioritized goal.

» First, the anecdotal evidence of climate change continues to mount and to be linked to the reality of people's lives. Ice caps are abstract, polar bears less so, and extreme weather even less so. The photos of snow-bound cars stranded on the streets of Washington, D.C., on five separate occasions in the winter of 2010–11 begin to seem as close to home as a car chase on the evening news. Severe weather advisories are drawing record viewers to their television sets. It may sound a bit light, but it is the stuff of public opinion.

» Second, the younger generations in the United States—the Xs, the Ys, and the millennials—are much greater believers in climate change than their predecessors. As they become the editors, CEOs, and senators of tomorrow, the segment of the debate focused on whether climate change is really happening is likely to become moot.

» Third, there is substantial evidence that Xs and Ys can shift the country's paradigms in a very short time. For example, from 1995 to 2011 there has been such a dramatic shift in gay rights—driven by Xs and Ys—that we can scarcely remember the country's former frame of mind. What was a deeply polarizing issue has transcended partisan politics. The unimaginable hurdles of marriage and military service for gay men and women now seem more like just a matter of time and due process. The system can shift its goals and paradigms in relatively short order.

Many influential thinkers are making efforts to shift our system goals and telling more compelling stories than we could hope to in this book. Our interest lies in how to shift the *behavior* of the system with the best possible side effects: How can we change our emissions profile with low short-term impact on our GDP and a large positive long-term impact on the national and global balance sheet? It is critically important that we find a path of action that minimizes economic cost and maximizes innovation, delight, and resiliency. The lower the hurdle, the sooner public opinion can shift enough to push us over it. This book therefore focuses on the second group of leverage points that Meadows describes—those related to metrics, information flows and feedback loops, parameters and rules within the system. We refer to these collectively as "frameworks."

Changing Climate System Frameworks

Many of the efforts thus far on energy efficiency and carbon emissions reduction have been doomed, not because they weren't earnest enough, or creative enough, or appealing enough, but quite simply because they took place in a framework that destined them to fail. Carbon emissions are a new type of problem that is at once abstract and systemic. Conversely, climate stability is a public good with no history of public policy tools to protect it. We have made disappointingly little progress because we have pushed on uncoordinated strategies in a system whose equilibrium has absorbed all our energy and prevented us from having an impact. It's as if we're punching with all of our strength into a wall of jelly and wondering why we're not connecting in any kind of satisfying way. Why is the framework failing us? There are three key factors:

»   Our laws and regulations are full of barriers to innovation around energy use.
»   We have no tradition of how our institutions can work together on this problem.
»   We have not ascribed an economic value to climate stability.

With these obstacles in place, all of our efforts are destined to have minimal impact at best. Without changing the framework, it's hard to imagine people working on climate change in a way that is aligned and cumulative. This book is about how to fix the frameworks that impact our buildings, land use strategies, and transportations systems, which are all interrelated and which collectively account for 77 percent of global, man-made carbon emissions.[5]

A great deal has been written about the patterns of development that would result in lower energy use and carbon emissions. There are books on lowering carbon emissions in cities, neighborhoods, new buildings, upgraded buildings, bicycle networks, and transit systems, among other topics, but they contain remarkably little about *how we can change our frameworks* so that all of these efforts can thrive and have a meaningful impact. The Urban Land Institute, the Rocky Mountain Institute, the U.S. Green Building Council, to name just a few organizations, have done essential work in articulating a vision for where we are trying to go—in other words, for what kinds of outputs our system should have. As a result of their efforts, we understand the impact that compact urban development, better mobility systems, and building design improvements can have on the nation's carbon emissions. Their efforts and those of countless others have laid out a vision that is compelling, and one whose impact on emissions is quantitatively validated.

But those who have sought to bring this vision to life have faced countless challenges. Developers face daunting obstacles to redevelopment of underutilized urban land. Architects in the United States face building codes and other regulatory impediments to energy-saving designs that have become routine practice in European cities. Even investors who are motivated to support lower carbon buildings and neighborhoods face increased risks and lower returns. Why have we ended up in a system where sound business judgment consistently points us away from our emerging system goals? How can we all start rowing in the same direction and in the same rhythm so that we can actually get somewhere? How can we create a system that has less dramatic tradeoffs between its current goals (making money, being happy) and its emerging one (stabilizing climate)? If we can lower the cost of trade-offs by improving how our system functions, we may not have to wait until the situation is totally dire before we start to make progress on climate change.

When it comes to carbon efficiency, society's institutions are like a child learning to swing. They pump their feet and rock back and forth, but the swing is going nowhere. We need to learn to feel when to bend our knees and when to straighten them. We need to know when to tip back and when to sit up. If we can find a way to coordinate all these small motions, each pump of the legs will be cumulative with the last, and soon we can be swinging very high with little effort. Swinging is a simple metaphor for what we need to do. Knowing we need a framework for coordinated action is one thing, and articulating that framework in its entirety is quite another. In just the same way that reconciling an entire government budget is a far cry from single-issue lobbying, so articulating a carbon-efficient framework for the built environment is quite different from understanding the viability of green roofs.

What does it mean, anyway, to be *carbon-efficient*? A carbon-efficient economy is one that emits as little carbon as possible while still providing people with the greatest possible choice and value. Our economy is already efficient in financial terms; what if we eliminated barriers to profitable low-carbon development strategies? If we did this, we would be on a path to a carbon-efficient economy. If we can create a framework that promotes carbon-efficiency, all of our economic energy and ingenuity can be put to work giving people even more choices than today and at the same time dramatically reducing the country's carbon footprint.

This book is about how we get there. It's not about the vision or the goals that so many others are laboring on. It's also very deliberately not just about *one* of the things we need to do. It's about creating a regulatory and economic environment in which the DNA of sustainable buildings and cities can be successfully expressed. It's about all the signposts we need to realign and about changing the path of least resistance to what we really want it to be. It is a thorough revisiting of how our institutions are leading us astray, and a set of tools to help us fix them. Although the book focuses on buildings and cities, many of its approaches are just as relevant to the good work being done on vehicle design, alternative generation, and industrial processes.

With new frameworks our economy can function more efficiently in how it uses money and generates CO_2. We can have more innovation, more choice, and more productivity. Ten chapters that follow are a distillation of key principles from the literature on lower carbon buildings and cities. In each case we identify where we are trying to go at the beginning of the chapter. Each chapter then goes on to look at how existing economic frameworks would need to be adapted to make that vision possible in a massive and general way across the economy. Some of the systemic barriers are small, in a why-didn't-we-think-of-that-sooner kind of way, but others are more politically challenging.

Why include suggestions that may be politically prickly? Because as the system goals evolve, we can tackle different parts of the solution. It's hard to predict the exact path that public opinion, business leaders, and elected leaders will take, so we've attempted to chart out all the key leverage points to support our evolving goals. If the United States wants to invest in insurance against climate change, we should buy the best insurance we can for the least amount of our GDP. The way to do that is to set market forces, innovation, ingenuity, and process efficiency to work on all aspects of the problem.

Perhaps more important, our dependence on burning fossil fuels is so entrenched in the economics of the system that the degree of change we need can only come from the transformative innovation and massive scaling that is possible in private markets. To get the market to gnaw on this bone, we need to take the (sometimes challenging) political steps that get capital flowing to the problem.

Ten Key Strategies

Both chaos and innovation are the seeds of success in the technological space of energy efficiency. Both are critical, but we have lacked a way to make sense of that chaos, to connect innovations and scale new technologies into mass adoption. The ten strategies described in this book point the way there. In summary, they are:

1   Create global measurement standards and accounting practices.
2   Develop enabling economic and technical frameworks.
3   Align regulatory mechanisms.
4   Reduce.
5   Reuse, restore, retrofit, and build quality buildings.
6   Focus on neighborhoods.
7   Include spaces for nature.
8   Foster on-site life cycles for water and energy.
9   Optimize transportation solutions on a regional scale.
10 Innovate for delight.

The structure of the chapters owes a debt to Christopher Alexander, who in *A Pattern Language* provides a set of tools for an essentially decentralized and organic transformation of buildings and cities. Although his focus was more on the aesthetics and human functionality of architecture, his framework is an excellent one for encouraging collaboration.[6] The opening of each chapter in this book outlines its central principle. This is followed immediately by examples of how the principle works (e.g., "Recognizing Effective Measurement" in chapter 1). The final section of each chapter gets down to the meat of the issue (e.g., "How We Can Improve Measurement"). Most suggestions are assigned to institutions within the U.S. economy, including governments, environmental nonprofits, and private sector businesses.[7] Other experts, such as Nicholas Stern, have dealt in depth with the frameworks required for international cooperation; the focus here is on what can be accomplished within the boundaries of one nation.[8]

Because climate change is such a new problem, we can find all too many examples of redundant and even counterproductive regulation implemented over the past few years at different levels of government. The underlying problem is that there is no tradition of appropriate level of agency. State governments know they have a mandate for education, and cities, school districts, and federal agencies know (more or less) how and who to coordinate with at the state level. But no such paradigm exists for carbon emissions and climate change. In each subject area, however, there are historical relationships that can point the way to the most effective jurisdiction for different institutions to truly coordinate their efforts. This, in turn, is critical. If the market is to focus its innovative and investment might on the problem, it needs not only the right sorts of signals, but also for those signals to be simple, predictable, and consistent.

This book strives to sort the signals from the noise and to give a comprehensive picture of "how we get there." It's a beginning of a roadmap. Doubtless, others will take it and add in missing streets or landmarks. What follows is a first and best effort at answering the questions of public policy makers, businesses, and the public: What do we need to do to make this happen?

CHAPTER 1

MEASURE FOR MEASURE

You can't manage what you don't measure.

—PETER DRUCKER

M easurement systems are symbolic representations of the real world. Effective measurement systems are standardized, verifiable, and widely adopted. This last qualifier is important: The value of a measurement system (or symbolic representation) as a communication tool increases as more people use it because the number of possible interactions that can leverage the measurement system goes up exponentially. If two people agree on a measurement based on the length of a maple leaf, it's not very useful to anyone who doesn't know the size of that leaf. But across the world, the length of a meter is a consistent measure that enables communication about length and distances among cultures and between people who have never met.

Atmospheric CO_2 gas, expressed in parts per million, is the widespread measure of the level of carbon in the earth's atmosphere. To reduce our carbon emissions, we also need to be able to measure our output at an emitter level. In recent years we have measured CO_2 output from processes in terms of pounds or tons of CO_2 per year. Figure 1.1 shows how global CO_2 production has increased since 1960 and the resultant change in CO_2 concentration in the atmosphere over the same period.

1.1. Annual total global CO₂ emissions and annual change in CO₂ concentration, 1960–2009. *Source:* http://www.worldclimatereport.com/index.php/2009/04/30/what-you-cant-do-about-global-warming

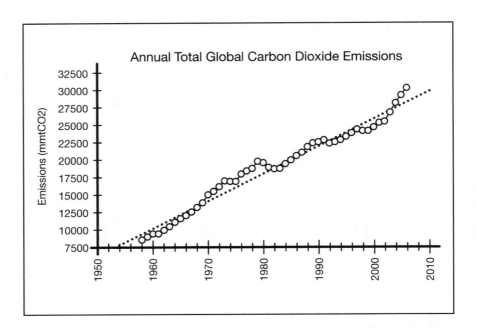

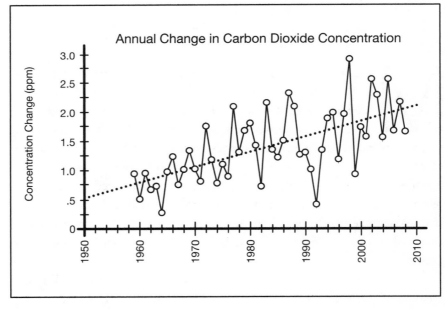

So far this is fairly simple, but it gets more complicated. Monitoring the amount of gas emitted by every activity from breathing to lighting a campfire is not feasible; we can't install a meter on everything in the world. The more practical solution is to monitor some fundamental processes in a controlled environment—for example, the burning of a liter of oil—and then create models to reflect the CO_2 emissions of real-life activities. What is most important is that everyone uses the same measurement system, the same process boundaries, and the same models so that we can communicate clearly and efficiently about carbon outputs. In reality, models aren't perfect. Near-perfect models—ones that reflect all of the variability and nuance of the real world—are too big and complex to be computationally tractable and too large to be easily verifiable by observation. More important than the need for perfection is the need for a model that is basically correct, that measures what we really want to change, and that is widely adopted.

If a model is widely used, communication happens easily and quickly. Putting this into economic terms, a standardized CO_2 measurement system will lower transactional costs between people using the model, because they can quickly come to a common understanding. Furthermore, if everyone adopts a standard measurement system or model, it can be refined over time as more and more people become conversant in the science and technology surrounding carbon emissions. If everyone is focused on refining *one* model for measuring CO_2, efforts will be directed in a cumulative and efficient way into improving that standard.

RECOGNIZING EFFECTIVE MEASUREMENT

A simple example of a standard that improves transactional and communication efficiency is the metric system. Across most parts of the world standard metric units are incorporated into other systems and models. This has simplified communication about these systems and models around the globe because virtually all countries use the same metric system as their standard. By contrast, for many Americans operating in the international arena, the United States's failure to adopt the metric system provides a daily object lesson in the inefficiencies of operating with a unique system that other players do not employ.

Of course, the metric system is a fundamental unit of measurement, so it doesn't have some of the modeling issues that other more complex systems of representation face. The challenge in modeling a highly variable situation with a simple system can be seen in a look at commodities trading. If we tried to use a model that accounted for the vagaries of each pig or each pound of coffee or each pound of frozen orange juice, there would be too much information about each unit to make trading efficient. Commodities markets work because the units they use are standardized. Investors trade frozen pork bellies, the commodity measure used for commercial supplies of bacon and other pork products, in contracts representing exactly forty thousand pounds of twelve- to eighteen-pound frozen bellies.[1] Enterprises that subsequently take physical delivery of the pork have an agreed system for making minor price adjustments that correspond to the specific characteristics of the physical items they receive. The market functions efficiently because everyone dealing in pork futures trades in it. While some pig farmers would undoubtedly argue that the uniform metric fails to capture the unique and valuable characteristics of the pigs they raise, the standard is indispensible because it provides a common ground in a way that multiple markets for different types and sizes of pigs could never achieve.

It is always tempting, in light of the imperfections of almost any standardized system, for organizations to decide that they need to come up with a version more tailored to their particular situation. Generally, however, the benefits of having a slightly more "perfect" model do not outweigh the advantages of the common standard in its communicative efficiency and its ability to continuously improve over time. For example, in 2007, King County in Washington determined that its State Environmental Policy Act (SEPA) process needed to include a system for evaluating projects in the built environment according to their greenhouse gas emissions. This was a move in response to political targets set at the state level for curbing emissions. The county spent several months engaging stakeholders from industry and government in developing a measurement and goal system for embodied, operational- and transportation-related emissions from the built environment. Throughout the process the stakeholders struggled with balancing their model's accuracy with its complexity. There was also significant concern about the additional reporting burden the new county model would impose on the private sector, as well as the additional administrative and review burdens that the county would impose on itself.

In the end King County wound up providing an alternate review and reporting path whereby if a project met the existing Leadership in Energy and Environmental Design (LEED) Gold standards, it was deemed energy-efficient (and carbon-efficient) enough to be meeting the state's targets. Stakeholders became comfortable with using the LEED Gold standard when they reviewed performance data on past projects and concluded that LEED Gold buildings *did* in fact perform at energy efficiencies that met the county and state targets. Despite the challenging targets set by LEED Gold, developers were relieved to avoid one more layer of reporting costs, and the attendant lag time while the county reviewed the data. A corollary benefit is that LEED undergoes continuous improvement with the help of many more resources than the county could ever marshal over time. As a result, the LEED standard has the potential to evolve and remain up to date in a way that the county's reporting mechanisms could never hope to achieve.

On the flip side, the absence of a clear, shared standard is not merely inefficient; it can actually lead to flawed comparisons and false conclusions. An article that first appeared in the *Wall Street Journal* in 2008 provides a classic illustration of the current lack of standards for quantifying carbon emissions.[2] Reporter Jeffrey Ball undertook a review of six consumer products to understand their true life-cycle carbon impact. He came up with the results summarized in table 1.1.

Life-cycle analyses vary in what they measure, but they generally include all the carbon impacts associated with production, transportation, operation, and disposal of a product. What is most important when comparing life-cycle

Table 1.1.

Reported Lifetime CO_2 Footprints of Six Consumer Products

Item	Lifetime CO_2 Footprint (lbs)	Major CO_2-producing component
Midsize sedan with 120,000-mile lifetime	126,000	Fuel consumed in use
Pair of leather slip-on boots	121	Leather
Laundry detergent to wash twenty loads of laundry (including water and energy)	31	Not specified
Polyester jacket	66	Polyester fabric
Gallon of milk in a plastic jug	7.2	Emissions from cows
Sixpack of bottled beer	7	Refrigeration in store

SOURCE: Ball, "Six Products, Six Carbon Footprints."

impacts is to use a consistent modeling methodology; otherwise, the comparison from one product to another is meaningless. In his introduction Ball noted that "different companies are counting their products' carbon footprints differently, making it difficult for shoppers to compare goods."[3] Ball attempted to normalize the results, but he found the different standards that had been applied made it all but impossible. In some cases disposal was considered, in others not. In the case of milk, the CO_2 generated in producing the feed consumed by the cows was not counted. It's easy to see how such an article, intended to make consumers more educated and aware, succeeds mainly in showcasing the complexity of the problem, because there is no standard for how we measure or model life-cycle emissions from consumer products.

HOW WE CAN IMPROVE MEASUREMENT

STRATEGY #1: Adopt a national standardized model and accounting practices for measuring greenhouse gas emissions as a necessary building block for managing a carbon-efficient economy. Support evolution of national standards and align them with emerging international standards.

Federal Government

Adopt the leading system in the market—even if it's not perfect—in developing policy, incentives, or regulation.

Given that the value of a measurement system is derived largely from the network of the effect of being shared among many users, it makes sense that there is a role for the federal government to play; many other important shared standards from generally accepted accounting practices (GAAP) to nutritional labeling of foods operate at a national scale and benefit from a national platform. The federal government is also the connection point to international goals and initiatives. When a federal government is a signatory to a treaty that sets goals for greenhouse gas emissions, there is an implied measurement system that the signatories can use to account for and demonstrate their success. The federal government is the natural body to translate international goals to meaningful national and regional targets.

Thus far, international emissions targets have tended to be relative, as in "by 2050, emissions will be reduced to 80 percent of 1990 levels." This sort of relative target has the benefit of being easy to scale. If we want the world's emissions to be reduced to 80 percent of 1990 levels, we can also hold each country or region to that standard. The problem with this type of scaling, however, is that population and economic activity in different countries and regions are changing, with some experiencing more rapid growth than others. Converting the target to a per capita number might be possible, but if we want to be able to really manipulate data effectively and correct for a variety of variables, we need information about absolute emissions.

At a macro-level, carbon markets in Europe have adopted standard assumptions about the emissions related to different activities and energy transformation processes. At a micro-level, the science around modeling the energy use and emissions from buildings is growing more detailed and more standardized every day. Federal governments need to work together globally and quickly to converge on these standard measurement systems as they emerge and use them to translate international goals into national, regional, and local goals. As the federal government creates incentives or regulation to reduce emissions, the ability of the economy to assimilate and respond to this change will be substantially affected by how quickly and consistently it is able to apply measurement tools that link the micro and macro analysis together. Even if a measurement system emerges that is not perfect, it is likely more effective to engage in supporting and influencing it rather than to create an alternate system with all of the attendant "translation" costs.

Establish clear national goals for carbon emissions and subgoals for smaller time intervals and regions.

Another way in which the federal government can play an important role in encouraging standardized measurement is to articulate a breakdown of large-scale targets into smaller geographic regions and time increments. To this point, most of the regional target-setting within the United States has been done from the bottom up, either by states and multistate alliances such as the Western Climate Initiative or by municipalities, often through vehicles like the Conference of Mayors. These grassroots efforts are important, but the federal government has the ability to generalize these goals across the whole country—avoiding first-mover disadvantages to regions that choose to act.

Equally important, they can create a framework that aggregates the contributions of different regions and improves understanding of how the country as a whole is meeting broader global targets. In the business environment the mnemonic PDCA (plan, do, check, act) is frequently used to describe the

Table 1.2.

Steps Required to Establish a National Standard Greenhouse Gas Measurement System

PLAN	Adopt and support the standard measurement system. Set national and regional targets in absolute terms and with time horizons.
DO	Implement appropriate legislation and policy to send signals to the market about the application of the standards.
CHECK	Track progress on targets; evaluate how evolving measurement tools are impacting adequacy of goals and progress.
ACT	Tweak policy levers to clarify market signals.

standard and goal-setting process.[4] The actions required of the federal government in support of standard measurement systems, broad goal setting, and subgoal articulation is depicted in table 1.2.

State and Local Governments

Adopt national standards so that companies can innovate and reap the benefit at a national scale.

State and local governments also need to adopt the common standard. They are in a unique position to provide feedback about where the measurement standard is failing in practice. Without doubt, refining the measurement system will take time, and initially there will be gaps between the model and the reality that can skew incentives if appropriate adjustments are not made.

Provide feedback to the federal level.

State and local governments also need to provide feedback about what regional subgoals are most appropriate. Even with a system of measurement that has the clarity of absolute numbers, there will be (and needs to be) intense debate about what other economic and social goals are to be balanced with emissions targets. This discussion is rife with potential for clashes among local interests—state governments will play a crucial role in deciding how these issues get arbitrated.

Environmental Nonprofits and Private Sector Companies

Generate standards, adopt leading standards, and monitor their integrity.

Nonprofits and businesses, not government, are in the best position to develop a measurement system. Many important measurement systems have come out of the nonprofit research community and the private sector, where actors are driven by the need to pursue a goal in the most efficient way possible and to convey an idea quickly and simply to clients or the public. It is difficult to overstate the enormity of the contribution made by the nonprofit International Organization for Standardization through its 18,500 international ISO standards covering everything from agriculture to information technology.[5] The U.S. Green Building Council (USGBC) has developed the LEED certification standard mentioned earlier, which is now a leading indicator of sustainable buildings, campuses, and neighborhoods. In both cases the rating systems have been successful for a few different reasons:

» They have built strong brand recognition, so that people who want to use the information don't have to replicate the analysis, but rather can trust the result.

» They have been refined over time in response to changes in the practices of the analyzed entities (companies and buildings).

» They are seen as an independent, and therefore trustworthy, verification process.

As a cautionary note, private sector rating systems run the risk of becoming subservient to their parent organization's short-term interests. In the long term, maintaining an up-to-date and reliable measurement and accreditation system serves the rating agency well, but there are always short-term motivations to secure a customer, to reach a political goal, or to meet quarterly earnings that can compromise the impartiality of measurement systems and ratings. Although nonprofits are less likely to be at the cutting edge of the market, and therefore tend to have systems that lag the market somewhat, they may also be less subject to these profit-driven temptations. When the originator of the measurement system is a private sector company, nonprofits have an important watchdog role to play in reviewing the accreditation and measurement methodology and keeping it true to broader societal goals.

The central tenet of this chapter is that there should be one standard metric for measuring greenhouse gas emissions. By definition, that means that while many for-profit and nonprofit companies may influence the standard, few of them will actually be involved in its creation. Enterprises in general can, however, support the standard to their long-term benefit. A good example of an industry that came to this realization rather slowly is the franchise hotel business. A small number of major hotel chains and their subsidiary flags account for a large portion of this market. Over the past several years some chains realized that their customers were becoming more informed consumers of sustainable retail products and experiences. Some observers suggested that hotels should use the existing LEED standards for buildings to demonstrate their commitment to sustainability to their guests.

Many hotel chains, however, initially avoided jumping on this band-wagon. Like most good, skeptical businesses, they were worried about applying a measurement system meant for buildings to their own type of assets—build-ings and operating businesses rolled together. They were concerned about being constrained by a measurement system that might lead them to do things that their clients wouldn't value. If your customers consistently tell you that the quality of the "shower experience" is part of why they come back, it seems a risky proposition to consider a rating system that may push you toward low-flow shower heads. As a result, the hotel companies initially rejected LEED, announcing instead that they were going to come up with their own internal sustainability initiatives and measurement systems. Savvy customers quickly realized that without a standard third-party rating or measurement, any hotel could claim that it was "sustainable," and a hotel's use of the term didn't really mean anything they could rely on. The self-determined hotel sustainability ratings didn't gain any traction in the market, and hotels have now turned to working with the USGBC on a LEED standard for hotels. Because its brand is now widely understood and trusted, the LEED-based approach is earning real support from hotel customers.

Promote measurement systems and results.

The Center for Neighborhood Technology (CNT), in collaboration with the Center for Transit Oriented Development (CTOD) and with the help of the Brookings Institute Urban Markets Initiative, has developed a more comprehensive way of thinking about affordability of housing by calculating the transportation costs associated with a home's location. Their H+T index includes all travel (including commuting) that is part of a typical household daily routine as well as the cost of housing. It has been expanded to cover 337 metro areas with the assistance of the Rockefeller Foundation and several other nonprofits in specific urban centers.[6]

In March of 2009 the U.S. secretaries of Housing and Urban Development (HUD) and the Department of Transportation jointly announced the creation of an interagency partnership to promote sustainable communities through coordinating housing and transportation policy and investments. CNT's work was cited several times in their testimonies to demonstrate the key relationship between housing affordability and transportation costs.[7] This is an excellent example of the powerful influence nonprofits can have when they work together to develop and promote credible measurement systems that create a rationale for action by governments.

Educational and Research Institutions

Test and provide feedback on the operational performance of standards.

Educational institutions often play a role similar to that of nonprofits in reviewing the accounting and measurement methodologies of other entities. Academic and research environments have an important role to play in examining measurement tools to make sure that they realistically calibrate the impact of lower-carbon strategies. Their own measurement and management methodologies can inform the development of national measurement strategies and can help refine them with emerging data. Higher education institutions also often have a unique opportunity to serve as a controlled testing ground for new models of measurement and emissions regulation. Campus-wide CO_2 reduction schemes can be a good proxy for trying out neighborhood strategies. The results of these campus-wide efforts can calibrate models beyond the "energy-efficient building" level to incorporate broader district energy, land use, transportation, and access impacts.

As an aside, in the field of sustainability, educational institutions have been leaders in doing as well as in thinking, in part because energy efficiency made strong economic sense for them. The public-entity status of K–12 schools, as well as some higher education institutions, means that their capital and operating budgets are separated by law. While capital budgets can be replenished in good times through bonds or levies, operational budgets are perennially constrained. This has meant that many educational institutions have been early adopters of energy-saving technologies, particularly building retrofits that leverage performance contracting by energy services companies (ESCOs). ESCOs guarantee energy cost saving from improvements in the physical plant, and the investment is paid back over time from the cost savings from lowered energy use. A number of educational institutions have engaged in this type of energy retrofit for buildings to free up operational funds. They are early adopters of a lower-carbon model, and many of them have good data and experience measuring the return on investment that can be achieved.

MEASUREMENT IN A NUTSHELL

As the example from the *Wall Street Journal* article so emphatically illustrates, we are a long way from adopting a standardized approach to measuring carbon emissions. Doing so is a prerequisite to managing them—correcting this problem is one of three fundamental requirements for achieving a carbon-efficient economy (the other two are discussed in the next two chapters). Coordinated national standards have been implemented in many other areas of the economy, and a similar effort with respect to CO_2 emissions is both possible and urgently required.

CHAPTER 2

THE INVISIBLE HAND

I am learning that if I just go on accepting the framework for life that others have given me . . . I will be unable to recognize that which I have the power to change.

—LIV ULLMANN

Measurement systems are a fundamental building block for managing change. However, even visionary goals articulated in terms of concrete measurement systems do not create change on their own. Transforming our high-carbon economy to a successful low-carbon economy will require not only standardized measurements but also enabling frameworks that allow market forces to work in an efficient way.

What is an enabling framework? At its most basic level it is a coordinated approach that allows institutions to align their efforts. Where a measurement system is fundamental (like an alphabet or numbers), an enabling framework sits on top and allows people to work together in more complex ways (like language or calculus). Enabling frameworks are often so ingrained in human enterprise that we don't even notice them. This can make them difficult to think about. Before moving on to how enabling frameworks could transform our economy's carbon dependency, it may be helpful to consider some illustrative frameworks and the human activities they enable.

RECOGNIZING EFFECTIVE FRAMEWORKS

Money within country borders and currency exchange markets are an example of a framework that enables economic activity at a national scale and allows for international commerce as well. Currency markets make it possible for goods (and price signals) to flow across country borders, resulting in an integrated global economy. While tariffs and limited human mobility remain a significant distortion to free markets (evidence of these anomalies is illustrated by *The Economist's* "Big Mac Index," which compares the price of an identical good—a McDonald's Big Mac sandwich—in different countries), currency markets are still quite successfully enabling global markets, which in turn allows for specialization across economies and drives market share to low-cost and high-value producers.[1] As early as 1776 in *An Inquiry into the Nature and Causes of the Wealth of Nations,* Adam Smith referred to "the invisible hand" of economic frameworks guiding the behavior of individuals and businesses in our society.[2]

On the technical side, frameworks are equally important. Frequently in the technical world enabling frameworks are known as interfaces. Three-prong electrical outlets with 110-volt AC power are a standard framework that allows for versatility in the production and use of electrical appliances. The three-prong 110-volt interface is a critical part of the match between efficient infrastructure and a broad range of consumer appliances. Conversely, who hasn't encountered the angst of traveling with a cell phone and being required to buy a new charger to replace the one forgotten at home? Although we may finally see a common phone-end connection in the next few years, what economic inefficiency for the consumer who needs to purchase a new charger with each new phone and throw the perfectly functional old one away, or for the retailer who has to stock a whole rack of chargers, consuming inventory and space, when they all perform exactly the same function.[3]

Like measurement systems, frameworks gain value from standardization and universality. In the mid-1970s two competing technical frameworks emerged for video recording and replicating movies on tape for home use: VHS and Betamax. Despite its superior image quality and smaller tapes, Betamax didn't gain the market share that VHS did, primarily because in the early stages of the videotape format war the VHS standard was more versatile and could make longer recordings (an important advantage for recording Monday night football games). As a result, Betamax didn't gain a big enough market share to be price competitive, and VHS became the dominant technical framework for the next twenty years until the advent of DVDs.[4]

Without enabling frameworks, transactional costs and economic friction remain high. This in turn discourages innovation and adoption in technologies, processes, and business relationships. The frameworks we have talked about so far vary: all are rules or norms that govern relationships, but some are big-picture and allow for a great deal of variability and evolution (such as currency exchange markets), while others are highly specific and tangible (such as three-prong outlets). The specificity of frameworks is an important concept. The more specific it is, the more easily it is adopted, and the more it lowers transactional costs for all users. Frameworks in the form of simple and highly specific standards often have low technological and knowledge barriers. They tend to produce better results when large numbers of people adopt them, but they can be rigid and can limit innovation. On the other hand, broader, more complex, and more *results-oriented* standards are more difficult to implement, require more analysis, and are less efficient on a transactional basis, but they are much more supportive of innovation.

What does all this mean? Imagine you are building an airplane. So much information goes into building an aircraft that no single person can know it all. To make the technical problem manageable, airplane manufacturers break up the problem into component parts: the wings, the fuselage, the interior, the navigational equipment, and so on. Each team of designers and engineers works on a discrete piece that is delivered to interface in a specific way with the other pieces. For instance, the wing team knows the shape of the joint and the types of loads they can put on the fuselage at the joint. The fuselage team knows the shape of the joint and the maximum load from the wing that they need to bear. If both teams design to this interface, the parts will fit together perfectly when they are produced.

Now imagine that we build passenger airplanes like this for a hundred years. At some point the airplane can be improved only so far within that framework. Imagine next that somebody comes up with an idea for an airplane that looks more like an airfoil—one big triangle viewed from the top. But how do we implement this using the old interfaces? Where do the fuselage and wing teams begin and end their scope of work when the wing *is* the fuselage? This is not a hypothetical story. Before Boeing went ahead with its new 787 passenger airliner program, the company's engineers seriously considered an alternate program called the "blended wing body" (BWB), which held promise of being significantly more energy and fuel efficient.[5] Boeing had concerns about the hurdles a BWB aircraft would face related to passenger comfort and fit with current airport infrastructure. But many industry observers believe that the dramatic organizational reconfiguration that would have been required had Boeing attempted to redefine its standards and interfaces also played a significant role in the eventual decision to go with the more traditionally shaped 787 airplane.

The 787 relies on a design and production process that is disaggregated through the supply chain, with Boeing acting more as the final assembler than as an integrated producer. When the interfaces define not only how parts of an organization relate but also how different companies define their contractual relationships, they are solidified even further. Given how integral the current aircraft manufacturing framework has become to its entire business model, it is hard to imagine how Boeing will ever change it. The point of this story is to illustrate how highly standardized interfaces can create efficiency and allow for incremental change on either side of the interface (improvements to the wing, improvement to the fuselage), but also how they tend to constrain the type of change that might create a whole new architecture that produces value. The value of airplanes is not in wings and fuselages. The wings and fuselage are just artifacts of a means of getting people from one place to another quickly.

Design visionary Buckminster Fuller is often credited with the saying, "You never change anything by fighting the existing. To change something, build a new model and make the existing obsolete."[6] This is a key concept when thinking about how the world can change in response to climate change goals. Although some people may change their behaviors because they feel strongly that it is the right thing to do, the easiest way to get lots of people to change what they do in a substantial way is to give them a better alternative that creates more perceived value and delights them. For our country and our world to move to a productive and satisfying low-carbon economy, we need transformative innovation that delivers more value. While incremental improvements in airplane fuels and engine fuel efficiency are important, we may have more luck fundamentally transforming our carbon output if we focus on new ways to get people from one place to another quickly. Or at an even bigger-picture level, by asking ourselves: Why do they want to get from one place to another quickly? Is their real need better access to people they do business with or care about? There may be ways to produce that result that don't involve traveling at all.

The reason this is all so important is that policy development needs to reflect these two needs that are in tension with each other: the need for simple standards and frameworks that can be adopted easily, and the need for big-picture, results-oriented frameworks that allow for innovation. Only with results-oriented frameworks can innovators ask transformative questions about real need and customer value that allow us to rethink our buildings, land use paradigms, and transportation and access tools. Table 2.1 illustrates some of the key advantages and disadvantages of the two contrasting framework types, using as an example the requirement to reduce water runoff from new developments.

Now let's take a look at the enabling frameworks we need to get to an efficient and innovative low-carbon economy.

HOW WE CAN CHANGE FRAMEWORKS

STRATEGY #2: Create frameworks and interfaces that enable efficient economic transactions and that increase transparency about CO_2 emissions. Strive for a balance between specific standards for ease of adoption and results-oriented frameworks that create room for innovation.

Federal Government

Impose a tax on carbon and water (offset by income and business tax reductions) to send a clear signal through the supply chain.

Perhaps the most important framework adjustment we can make is to raise the price of energy. No other single strategy can send such a clear and pervasive signal to the market about the value of CO_2 reduction. No other strategy embeds the carbon impact of every product into its price.

It would be counterintuitive and counterproductive for a book that attempts to take a systems approach to climate change to not consider energy and freshwater resources as interdependent and limited public goods. A unilateral focus on carbon reduction would likely threaten our freshwater supplies even more than they already are today. A huge amount of water is used in the petroleum refining process; water is diverted in the generation of hydro-electricity; it is used to grow biofuels and in the manufacturing of all equipment that we use to transform and transmit energy. One of the newer solutions to freshwater shortages is desalination, which itself is incredibly energy intensive. The problem of dwindling freshwater reserves in many populated parts of

Table 2.1.

Simple Standards versus Results-Oriented Frameworks

The example is based on reducing water runoff from new development.

Attribute	Simple Standards	Results-Oriented Frameworks
Form of framework	Checklist.	Calculation tool or analytical method.
Example	Specifying three types or manufacturers of pavement that are allowable as "porous pavement" within the code.	Allowing any type of surface that can show an adequate level of infiltration or meet minimum runoff standards. Provide or adopt a standard tool to measure infiltration or runoff in the finished product.
Customer who benefits most	Homeowner renovating a driveway, or a developer of a small industrial project who has a tight budget and no staff or ability to redo calculations.	Larger developer with a constrained site or geography who needs to think out of the box to meet targets and make the project profitable. Alternately, an innovative pavement or surfacing company that develops a new product and wants to introduce it into the market.
Benefit to customer	Quick off-the-shelf solution.	Allows flexibility.
Long-term impact on costs	Encourages market adoption of products allowing for more efficient production and distribution.	Encourages innovation of better and lower-cost solutions.
Risk profile	Low risk, simpler for rules-based bureaucracies and institutions to deal with.	Higher risk, probabilistic measures of success. Some implementations may not work as modeled.
Liability profile	Limited liability.	Permits a broader view of liability that balances project risk with societal risk.
Potential to evolve over time	Can be updated as new technologies evolve to reflect the most effective choices (but confidence in the standard is undermined if it changes too often).	Strategies that demonstrate success through the calculation method can be incorporated into the simple standard or checklist method.

the world will likely be exacerbated by climate change and will soon threaten human habitation just as much as do rising sea levels. Two things are clear:

» Climate stability and adequate supplies of fresh water are *both* at risk.
» Their relative adequacy is interdependent.

Accordingly, proposed entrepreneurial approaches and public policy changes to reduce CO_2 emissions are intended to be sensitive to the need to balance water conservation with controlling greenhouse gas emissions. The value of federal government intervention in setting a price on water and carbon emissions is greatly debated, but there are four compelling reasons to impact price at this level of government. First, voluntary carbon reductions are not transforming the economy fast enough. Hoping that individuals and private enterprise will buy into carbon curbs or offsets at a pace that will impact global warming is akin to hoping that private enterprise will suddenly band together and repair the interstate highway system or provide adequate schooling to every child in the country.

Second, there is a game theory problem. So far, in the face of a vacuum of federal leadership on climate change, states and cities have gotten into the act. California has passed automobile emissions legislation and by sheer force of its market share has made many manufacturers move to their higher standard on all the cars they sell in the country. The U.S. Conference of Mayors Climate Protection Center has worked at coalescing grassroots efforts across the country around urban policy and planning that reduces carbon emissions.[7] However, there is a political cost to being the leader in voluntary carbon reduction. Every time a city or state raises the bar unilaterally on carbon emissions, it risks raising at least the perceived cost of doing business in that place. This puts the business community up in arms because their playing field isn't level any more. On the other hand, if markets change across the country as a whole, regional inequalities around carbon pricing are eliminated. Furthermore, producers can achieve economies of scale when one version of a product is required nationally.

Third, utilities, a major generator of CO_2, are regulated at the federal level. While chapter 3 focuses on this in greater depth, the signals sent by the regulatory environment need to be consistent with the pricing signals in the market. The best way to do this is to administer both at the same level of jurisdiction.

Fourth, to the extent that we are signatories to treaties setting goals with respect to emissions reduction, the country as a whole needs to meet these goals. Only at the federal level can progress be nationally monitored and pricing be adjusted accordingly.

A great deal of energy has been invested in discussion of "cap and trade" as a national system to lower carbon emissions. As is so often the case in these matters, this intense debate has generated more heat than light. The basic premise of cap and trade is that the government sets "caps" or limits on emissions for different emitters across the country. Emissions are monitored either by the emitters themselves (which is problematic) or by some third party (which is expensive), and emitters who are below their cap receive credits. Emitters who are above their cap can either implement solutions to reduce emissions or buy credits on an open market from the people who have them. Credits can also be sold into the market by voluntary reducers on the basis of carbon-offset projects—projects that have reduced emissions below the level where they otherwise would have been.

Market-based cap and trade was implemented in 1995 in the Acid Rain Program, an initiative enacted by the U.S. Congress to control emissions of sulfur dioxide (SO_2) that caused acid rain. Rather than regulating SO_2 emissions at a fixed level, the cap and trade system distributed "allowances" to emit SO_2 among regulated electric power plants. Plants with the lowest cost of reduction could take the lead and "bank" extra allowances to sell to those with a high cost of reduction, making the system economically efficient. The caps on total SO_2 from these sources were incrementally reduced over time, which gave the SO_2-emitting plants time to adjust their processes and technologies. It also allowed the lower cost/highest benefit strategies to be pursued first within an efficient market. The program has worked very well. With the final cap reduction achieved in 2010, total SO_2 emissions from power plants are equal to one-half the amount emitted in 1980.[8]

Unfortunately there are some fundamental differences between the SO_2 market in the 1980s and 1990s and the carbon emissions markets today. Nearly all of the big SO_2 polluters were industrial, which limited the number of monitoring points as well as the number of strategies that needed to be implemented. This is clearly not the case for greenhouse gas emissions. Registered vehicles alone create more than 250 million monitoring points in this country, and homes add another 125 million or so.[9] In addition, the market for SO_2 emissions was limited to a continent and a finite group and type of emitters, which allowed the offsets to be measured, understood, and ultimately commoditized in such a way that they could be efficiently traded. This experience is in stark contrast with the carbon dioxide cap and trade markets of Europe, which have been plagued with the problem of measuring and quantifying offsets. In particular, offsets explained in terms of "we avoided future emission by not doing the following" as opposed to actual investments in changing production technology are inherently difficult to quantify. As a by-product of this phenomenon, there is a perverse incentive for businesses to push for lax regulation and business standards so that they can show a large improvement over the regulation or base standard and create a large and lucrative (and fictional) offset.

Given all the challenges of cap and trade, we suggest a simpler system. The federal government should impose a flat tax on carbon and water. The proceeds of this tax should be entirely rebated through income and business taxes resulting in no net burden on the economy. We should probably take a break right here to let everyone catch their breath. Unquestionably, new taxes, even ones that are instantly put back into the hands of consumers and businesses, are always politically challenging (not only in the recent political climate) because they are very unpalatable to many sectors of the economy. The cap and trade idea has consequently gained more traction in recent years, probably because of its track record on SO_2 emissions, its perceived efficiency, and its general squishiness. It's hard for opponents to rally solid objections to something that has no clear path to implementation and that most people don't really understand. However, though the words *cap and trade* at first seem more benign than *carbon tax*, opposition to cap and trade increased sharply during 2010 in the United States as more and more people began to understand the many challenges involved in its implementation.

Keep net tax revenue constant: Rebate the proceeds to reduce taxes on economically productive activities.

Consideration of a carbon tax is still almost unthinkable to many. It's clear how a tax works, and the public is likely to have an instant negative reaction to a pervasive new levee like a carbon tax. Some economists also object, citing the concern that new taxes take money from productive uses where it can create value (i.e., businesses) and put it in the hands of government, where it is much less likely to stimulate economic growth. However, the proposed tax on carbon emissions and water use avoids that problem if it is entirely returned to productive uses immediately, as has been done with a carbon tax implemented in British Columbia in 2008.[10]

The real purpose of this tax is to create an economic disincentive to emitting carbon or consuming water, in the same way we create economic disincentives (such as taxes or fines) to other behaviors that negatively impact the public good. Although some have suggested that revenues from a carbon tax could be used to invest in "technical assistance" or "smart growth," the best avenue to making such a tax politically palatable is to return the money immediately to the productive and innovative parts of the economy (private enterprise and individuals) by lowering other taxes and letting them quickly get on with the business of innovating and making more informed choices.

It may also help to look at other examples of behaviors that negatively impact the public good that are already taxed. Many people may consider it a basic right to smoke and drink alcohol, but that does not stop the public from accepting that these activities should be heavily taxed. Our national consensus is that drinking, while allowable, can cause people to do foolish things that are not in the public interest. This makes the public comfortable with taxing alcohol sales and consumption. Smoking is an even better example. Over the past thirty years the science has become increasingly clear that smoking poses a significant health risk not just to smokers but to the people around them. Furthermore, as a society, we have become increasingly cognizant of the economic burden of paying for the higher health care costs of smokers. Our unwillingness to accept these burdens on the public good has created widespread acceptance for the taxation of cigarettes and other tobacco products.

Another often-raised objection to increasing the price of water or energy is that water, and perhaps some amount of energy, are basic human rights. We can't charge more for these, the argument goes, and in fact we shouldn't charge at all. It's a nice thought, but one that only works in a system with infinite resources. The reality is rather different: our energy and water resources, as well as our climate stability, are not only finite, they are threatened altogether. This begs the question of how to work out the social equity component of such a tax. One solution is to agree that we all have a right to a basic amount of clean water at a low cost. Above that threshold the price increases rapidly. This is not dissimilar to the system that has been implemented in many cities for garbage collection. With landfill space becoming increasingly scarce, a small amount of garbage is relatively inexpensive to dispose of, while a large amount leads to a hefty additional charge, an action, incidentally, that has been shown in one study in the Netherlands to reduce the amount of garbage produced per household by between 24 and 51 percent.[11]

Some cities and regions already include progressively higher pricing for above-average users of water and electricity, but the overall price discrepancy and the resulting price impact to high-volume users is still not big enough to consequentially change behaviors. Furthermore, we have not yet developed a good system to correct for household occupant density. Water, electrical, and garbage collection costs are all levied at a household level. In a sliding-scale rate system, this tends to penalize households with higher occupant densities, when in fact from a land use and household energy perspective we want to encourage more people to live close-in and closer together. A solution that addresses this problem might be to price all energy and water at the "high" rate and create a system of rebates for low-income users (in addition to receiving a share of the proceeds of the tax as an income tax credit, as proposed earlier). Canada has a functioning rebate program that sends quarterly credits to low-income citizens to offset a universal value-added tax that was implemented in 1991.[12] Another option might be to administer rebates like a food-stamp program, where individuals could put their "water stamps" toward a part of their water bill. In this system households with more occupants could pool more stamps to cover their water bill.

To put this in context, developers are often criticized for not doing enough to make their buildings energy efficient. Residential developers are also often reproached for not making their buildings more affordable. Even conscientious developers who want to do the right thing can't justify the investment—to themselves or their tenants—of significantly improving water and energy efficiency when operational costs are such a small fraction of the up-front cost of energy- and water-saving technologies. Only when there is a significant payback can the market adopt new technologies at a large scale. Only when energy and water are priced in a way that reflects their relative scarcity can "doing right" and "doing well" come into alignment for market participants. Only then can "affordable" and "efficient" really coexist in the same place.

If we implement a relatively simple carbon tax, the entire economy can meet the challenge of reducing carbon emissions in a completely entrepreneurial and decentralized way. Every person and every business has a financial incentive to do better than average on their carbon emissions. Furthermore, every product we buy, every piece of food we eat, every service we enjoy, all have embedded information about their carbon efficiency, all tied together in that most simple of economic indicators: their price. That's the beauty of it: the price of everything will partially reflect the global warming impact that thing had in its production, distribution, and even its design and marketing. Locally grown foods become more price competitive, and riding a bicycle gets you a lower net tax rate. The public good of climate stability gets taken into account by every consumer and business in every one of their decisions while still preserving the array of choices that consumers demand.

Tax at the source.

Perhaps the most important reason to favor a tax over a cap and trade system is its relative efficiency of implementation. There are a relatively small number of points where energy comes into the market or into the electrical grid. Barrels of oil and natural gas pipelines are the two principal ways in which energy comes across the country's borders. We already have infrastructure in place to monitor this supply and the ability to impose taxes based on the combustion efficiency and CO_2 output of these commodities. Oil and natural gas collected within country boundaries that are headed directly to consumers (without being transformed to electricity) could be taxed at the level of the producing company.

The other key source of energy is the electrical grid. The principal generation sources of electricity for the grid are coal combustion, natural gas combustion, nuclear electric power, and hydroelectric power as shown in figure 2.1. The "other" category comprises only 5 percent of total electric power generation and includes wind power and solar power along with combustion of petroleum, wood waste, and various chemicals, and gases.[13] It would be relatively easy to administer a carbon tax that is correlated with the CO_2 emission of the applicable electricity generation process, because the vast majority of this power is produced from a relatively small number of locations. Each of these sources of energy could be taxed based on their carbon emissions at the level of the generating plant. Given that the non-CO_2-emitting generation methods are typically small scale and widely distributed, the focus of taxation would be coal and natural gas plants. There are just over two thousand of these plants across the country, making a point-by-point system of taxation relatively efficient to administer.[14]

Conversely, we can begin to imagine how challenging it would be to administer a carbon tax at the point of consumption if we think about the millions of points at which energy is used, including residential and commercial buildings, industrial sites, and all manner of vehicles. A carbon tax would undoubtedly work best if it were harmonized at a global level; implementing the tax only in certain countries creates significant challenges for trade in an intensely integrated global economy.[15]

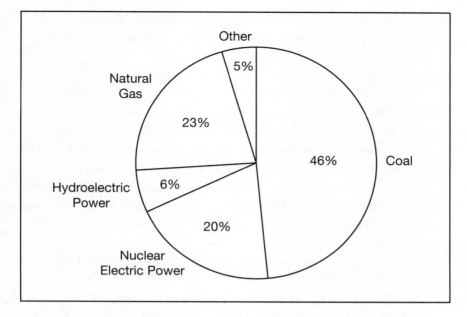

2.1. Sources of electric power in the United States, 2008. Source: U.S. Energy Information Administration

Take measures to ensure the carbon tax does not create a market disadvantage.

In the absence of a global carbon tax, the playing field between products produced inside and outside the United States will need to be leveled. It may be appropriate, as trade treaties allow, to levy a tariff on imports from countries that have a relatively low cost of emitting carbon. Conversely, to keep exports competitive, it may be necessary to rebate some of the tax to companies that export products that are high in embodied carbon to other countries that have low cost of carbon emissions. This is a risky business, however, because a system of tariffs that is manageable will never be perfectly reflective of embodied carbon. Furthermore, opening the door to tariffs also opens the door to protectionist interests that in turn could have huge impacts on global trade efficiency. In the end the consideration of tariffs may best be used as a negotiating tool by the federal government to gain leverage in agreements to harmonize a global carbon tax to the greatest extent possible.

Price water appropriately.

Earlier we alluded to the challenge of pricing water as well as carbon. If water is not priced properly, forms of energy and/or processes that are less carbon intensive but use more water may proliferate. A simple example of this would be the use of more water in an industrial process to avoid consuming power for cooling. Although a comprehensive solution to water shortages is beyond the scope of this book, it is clear that if we raise the price of emitting carbon, we also need to raise the price of water. Federal coordination is critical to avoiding game theory disincentives in this area as well. At the same time, policy needs to respond to the fact that water supply is regionally and seasonally dependent. In addition to pricing signals, some of the following tools may be useful to maintain a balance between water and energy efficiency:

» Establish federal policies to benefit states that make efficient use of water.
» Revise and harmonize state-level water rights laws to support more consistent management and conservation.
» Examine a location-based component to the price of water that reflects its scarcity in that location and the price of distribution to that location.
» Develop local pricing models that discourage additional development in fundamentally unsustainable areas and incent increases in the efficiency of existing building stock. At the same time, be aware of the need to grandfather in existing communities in high water cost areas.

Manage through the transition cost.

Even with a carbon tax that keeps net taxes constant, many economists have concerns that changing the structure of the tax base (and increasing the tax burden on a key economic resource like energy) can have transition costs. They believe that although the economic effect over the long term may be neutral, there are significant costs to individuals and industries adapting during the transition period to a less carbon-intensive or energy-intensive economy. There is some debate about how big this transitional effect would be and whether it could create economic distortions. One possible (and admittedly fairly radical) solution would be to invest the Federal Reserve with the ability to price carbon emissions: in other words, to set the carbon tax rate. The administration of the tax (and the leveling with other taxes to keep the net tax burden constant) would rest with the Internal Revenue Service.

Increasing the tax on carbon would have a slight dampening effect on the economy (similar to a twenty-five or fifty basis point interest rate hike). But unlike an interest rate hike, its effect would dissipate over time. A hike in the carbon tax (even keeping net taxes constant) could be used to dampen an over-heating market, or could be implemented in concert with an interest rate cut to keep the effect neutral. Over time, the effect of a carbon tax hike would disappear as the economy adapted and became more carbon efficient, and the Federal Reserve could go back to using primarily interest rates as a way of managing economic growth and inflation.

State Government and Local Governments

State and local governments live in a world of built-environment frameworks: building codes, zoning and land use codes, transportation and highway funding schemes, parks administration—the list goes on and on. Governments spend a good deal of their time creating these frameworks, defending them, altering them, and enforcing them. Subsequent chapters list dozens of frameworks that will need to change, some quite substantially, if we are to build a carbon-efficient economy. A small subset includes such things as managing all modes of transportation spending on a regional basis in a coordinated manner, adjusting zoning to support greater density, and putting a much greater focus on green spaces in urban areas to make them more attractive places to live in. In making the many changes outlined in this book, state and local governments should not lose sight of the fact that we will need to make a *large and coordinated set of adjustments* to our frameworks—not piecemeal change—to achieve success.

Developers and Other Private Sector Companies

Governments are not the only creators of economic frameworks. Private enterprise has its own set of generally accepted practices in the form of standard leases, standard compensation packages, and other types of standardized contracts and norms. While many business practices are explicit and subject to ongoing value engineering and cost reduction, sometimes it is difficult to see that an old way of doing business doesn't make sense in a carbon-efficient world. Some of the framework changes we propose for the private sector in subsequent chapters will require a reexamination of our old ways. Private sector players will need to think seriously about new possibilities for creating shareholder and stakeholder value. In addition to this "internal" aspect of the question, the framework adjustments that governments will be required to make to achieve a carbon-efficient economy will affect developers, investors, and other private sector companies, in some cases quite dramatically. The private sector has a responsibility to act as a constructive partner in this process.

FRAMEWORKS IN A NUTSHELL

It often requires painstaking effort to establish effective frameworks, but they are the organizing force enabling human collaboration. Not surprisingly, once they are in place, frameworks can be difficult to change. Subsequent chapters discuss dozens of frameworks on which our current high-carbon economy is founded; we will need to adapt them if we are to significantly improve our carbon efficiency. The most fundamental and dramatic change required is raising the price of energy through a carbon tax.

CHAPTER 3

REGULATORY ROADBLOCKS

Regulations grow at the same rate as weeds.

—NORMAN RALPH AUGUSTINE

C hapter 1 dealt with creating measurement and accounting standards for carbon emissions so that we could effectively measure carbon outputs. Chapter 2 talked about how getting technical and economic frameworks right can lead to efficient markets that ascribe real value to energy, water, and climate stability. Chapter 3 addresses the issues raised by the lack of alignment in the regulatory environment and the critical role that updated and consistent public policy can play in catalyzing a carbon-efficient economy. Carefully crafted regulation can have a salutary effect, but it is definitely not a panacea; the premise of this book is that efficient markets are the best path forward to scalable climate change solutions. Nonetheless, we live in a highly regulated world. Unfortunately, many of the regulations that exist today were crafted in a time when we were not aware of climate change, and many stand in the way of solutions to the problem.

What does it mean to align regulatory mechanisms? It means that we revisit our existing regulations, determine where they create barriers to a carbon-efficient economy, and revise them so that regulated entities work in concert with market forces rather than against them. There are all too many examples of cities, counties, and states trying to create "incentives" for developers, investors, and private sector companies to "adjust" their market interest. The City of Seattle, for instance, offers developers extra value in the form of additional floor area ratio (FAR) beyond zoning allowances when they build LEED Silver buildings. The Washington State Department of Ecology devotes considerable effort to crafting technical assistance programs for businesses that want to reduce their pollutant emissions. If the system were instead restructured so that doing the right thing made economic sense—if LEED Silver were more profitable than LEED Certified, for example—then piecemeal incentives would no longer be necessary.

RECOGNIZING EFFECTIVE REGULATION

The challenge that is created by the cacophony of regulation is illustrated in a simple story that would be amusing if it weren't so frustrating. In 2009 and 2010, Starbucks held two "cup summits," bringing together a wide range of stakeholders to identify actions they could take to achieve a goal of making 100 percent of their cups reusable or recyclable.[1] Starbucks estimates it will take until 2015 to achieve this milestone. The timetable is driven not by the technical issues of creating a watertight, cool-to-the-touch recyclable product, but rather by the astonishing variation in what is considered "recyclable" around the United States and the developed world. Even in Puget Sound, Starbucks's home base, the task is fraught with obstacles because of differences in local regulations; you can currently recycle the cup in Seattle but not in the suburb of Bellevue. In some cities, like Los Angeles, you can recycle the cup but not the plastic lid; if you take your coffee home, you can recycle the lid but not the cup.

The standards are often different in commercial and residential areas of the same city and can vary further depending on who the waste hauler is. In fact, in some jurisdictions, what is recyclable is defined by the local waste management company, not the local government. Variations like these occur from town to town across the country. As of mid-2011, Starbucks is making measured progress on this initiative through a variety of actions, such as working with local recycling agencies, providing front-of-store recycling bins, and offering discounts to customers who use reusable cups. They believe they are on track to achieve their 2015 goal.[2]

Perhaps the clearest example of regulation standing in the way of carbon efficiency is in how utilities are regulated. Utilities across the United States are incented to maximize generation capacity, sell the most power possible at the lowest possible price, avoid risk, and maximize predictability. While there is no question that a reliable power supply is a prerequisite to a strong economy, the stability and growth in the power supply needs to be regulated in a way that harmonizes with the need for carbon efficiency. Utilities may send out a newsletter to customers with "conservation suggestions" about switching from incandescent to compact fluorescent bulbs, but the regulatory environment pushes them to focus primarily on seeking newer, larger, and cheaper sources of power. On the one hand, utilities offer customers the option to pay a premium for clean sources of power; on the other hand, the federal government subsidizes the mining of coal, which is used to produce our dirtiest power.

The regulatory dis-synchrony doesn't end with utilities. In 2009 the federal government launched a popular economic stimulus program that was also meant to reduce vehicle emissions. The Cash for Clunkers program offered rebates to car owners who traded in a high-emissions vehicle for a more fuel-efficient one. At the same time, however, the federal government allocates funds to new state highways based on how much the citizens of that state are driving, effectively rewarding states with high per capita vehicle usage (and emissions) and fueling a cycle of traffic that begets more traffic. The federal government also divides roads and public transit into separate funding buckets, even though both roads and transit fulfill the same basic need—public mobility. To make matters worse, the approval thresholds for transit project funding are higher than those for new roads.[3]

There are conflicts between legislation and policy at the state level as well. In Washington State the Growth Management Act (GMA) encourages the development of compact communities, while the State Environmental Policy Act (SEPA) provides countless levers for disgruntled neighbors to thwart approval of higher-density projects. Mixed-use development at the neighborhood level, as discussed in more detail in chapter 6, maximizes the efficiency of travel between daily destinations, allowing residents to make many of their daily trips without the use of an automobile. This activates streets and other public spaces around the clock, making neighborhoods not only more pleasant but also safer and healthier. Local zoning regulation, however, generally continues to separate out land uses into distinct districts and neighborhoods.

Clearly, no level of our regulatory structure is immune from these conflicts, and this is perhaps not surprising, given how quickly our understanding of climate change has evolved. Regulation and legislation are comparatively slow to evolve. As they catch up, it's helpful to look for where barriers exist and remove them, rather than just piling on new regulations. A useful metaphor for this goal is the slalom ski course. Imagine a business is a skier, and the faster it gets down the hill, the greater the profit it makes. Imagine next that every piece of regulation is a pole, or gate, that the skier has to maneuver around. If you need the skier to be on one side or the other of the course at specific times, you can use gates to guide his path, but if the gates are too close together, the skier wastes energy and loses momentum. If you really want to have all those gates on the course, at least you can try grouping them so that the skier can get around them with fewer turns. Regulatory alignment is about grouping the gates efficiently and making sure that the skier doesn't have to hike uphill between them.

HOW WE CAN ELIMINATE REGULATORY ROADBLOCKS

STRATEGY #3: Establish an ongoing program to mitigate the current misalignment of legislation and regulation that is sending contradictory signals about carbon reduction to the market.

Federal Government

Create a level playing field through a consistently applied carbon tax and the elimination of piecemeal subsidies.

Within the current regulatory framework, some states and some utilities have tried to be innovative, frequently leaving themselves at a competitive disadvantage with respect to their neighbors in attracting industrial and technology users. A regulatory review at the federal level would set a level playing field across the country, eliminate the first mover disadvantage, and ultimately create a path to more efficient resource utilization for utilities and their customers.

Regulations also need to be harmonized with the proposed carbon tax and with existing subsidies for different forms of energy. Subsidies are expensive, skew the market, and have no economic multiplier effect when applied to mature technologies or industries. Regulatory reform should eliminate subsidies for mature technologies such as coal and oil. Subsidies of new technologies such as wind may be helpful in the short term but in all likelihood would be unnecessary if the playing field were leveled for new wind projects developed by utilities or by practically enabling distributed generation. Regulatory reform has the potential to be a driver of economic efficiency by eliminating the need for microincentives and subsidies, which cost taxpayers a great deal of money in direct and administrative costs. When implementing regulatory reform, we need to focus especially on eliminating incentives and subsidies that work at cross purposes with the goal of a carbon-efficient economy.

Align regulation of utilities to encourage conservation and distributed generation.

One of the most significant steps the federal government can take to harmonize the regulatory environment is to revise policies governing electric energy generation. Private and public utilities are not really incented to reduce consumption as a way of gaining capacity, nor are they properly enfranchised to leverage distributed generation as a reliable and significant share of the power supply.

There is strong evidence that a change in the expectation and regulatory environment for power producers can significantly impact the carbon efficiency of providing an adequate supply of power. Denmark was determined to improve energy self-sufficiency after being badly hit by the 1973 OPEC oil embargo. The initial response was to convert to coal-fired plants, but that led to levels of greenhouse gas emissions that concerned Danes. In the late 1980s Denmark implemented a program to encourage the development of wind power at the local level, and, perhaps most important, they have consistently stuck to this policy ever since.[4] In 1998 they adopted reverse metering, which allows any user who takes power from the grid to also feed energy back into it.[5]

These changes in the regulatory framework spawned technical developments. Wind turbines were not new technology, but their use was not widespread, and connecting them to the grid in volume presented new challenges. Reverse metering equipment, however, is proven, reliable, and widely available. To encourage participation, Denmark's utilities pay the distributed generators competitively for the power they put into the grid—producers are paid based on what users are willing to pay for "clean" power. (In many parts of the United States, utilities customers already have a choice to pay a premium for cleaner power, and many of them choose to do so.) Not only does Denmark provide distributed generators with a credit on their electrical bill for the power they generate, but if they are net producers rather than net users, they get a check at the end of the month. Finally, utilities are able to use their bonding capacity to help small generators finance their initial capital expenditures at advantageous rates. This further levels the playing field for distributed generation by making financing for small projects available as widely and cheaply as for large ones.

While there can be economies of scale in large-generation projects, it is worth remembering that transmission over long distances results in power losses and that new nuclear power plants in the United States cannot be developed profitably without either government subsidies or a significant carbon tax.[6] (Some plants that have been resold below cost, however, have proven profitable to the utilities that purchased them.) Although there have been programs to encourage the development of wind power in the United States, they have been plagued by inconsistency and on-again-off-again support.

As a consequence, many of the strategies available to Danish power producers and supporting industries are not possible at all, let alone at a large scale, for U.S. producers. The net result of revised and consistent utility regulation in Denmark is that after fifteen years, wind generation now produces power equal to 20 percent of Denmark's demand—most of it through distributed, small-scale generation.[7] As a by-product, Denmark has developed an international market leadership position in engineering and producing wind power systems, in sharp contrast with the state of the U.S. wind power industry. What changed in Denmark were the rules of the game, and much of this experience is transferable to the United States.[8] Altering the fundamental rules that govern how power is produced can do more than hundreds of piecemeal incentives for clean power or distributed generation.

Consider energy costs on a marginal cost basis to reflect the true benefits of energy-efficient technologies.

Right now utilities tend to think about their cost of energy on an "average cost" basis. They generally sell power at a price that is based on their average cost, meaning that the consumer price for energy is based on the average of the per unit cost of all of the sources of energy that a utility generates. When a utility buys power from another producer or adds new capacity of its own, it naturally tries to do so at a price that will not drive its average cost up. In a world where the next incremental unit of capacity costs about the same as all of the past capacity, this would be a reasonable way to look at it. However, in the United States we have already used up the capacity of most of our low-cost energy sources. For instance, the Hoover Dam was completed in 1936 and is a large power supplier to the states of Arizona, Nevada, and southern California.[9] While the Hoover Dam still has operations and maintenance costs, its capital costs are essentially paid off. That is, the power that it generates occasions only operational costs. In other words, power from the

Hoover Dam is cheap to produce. Power from a new wind farm in Iowa (or a new coal-fired power plant, for that matter) is comparatively more expensive because the price must not only cover operations and maintenance but also pay down the capital cost of the wind turbines.

Unless we make dramatic improvements in operating efficiencies, economic growth and new uses will continue to drive a need for additional power generation. If we want to reduce atmospheric CO_2, we would be wise to try to derive as much as we can of this new capacity from clean sources of power. However, as long as we continue to evaluate new power generation technologies against the average blended cost from existing sources, the new clean source is bound to seem uncompetitive. In pure economic terms, utilities should be indifferent to building new capacity at a given marginal cost and investing in energy-saving technologies at that same cost. Likewise, the marginal cost for utility-constructed capacity is the economically neutral price at which that utility should be willing to finance new distributed capacity. In other words, continuing to hold new external sources to the average-cost test puts new distributed generation or energy-efficiency projects outside the utility's walls at an unfair economic disadvantage to capacity increases by the utility. A change in regulation could alter that bias and create a level playing field, with positive economic impact (overall cost of power is cheaper) and positive carbon emissions impact.

State and Local Governments

Redefine the system boundaries in environmental quality standards.

Many state environmental policies were crafted during the 1970s and 1980s, and they still reflect that era in the way they look at automobile service levels. Ensuring capacity to move a lot of cars quickly is clearly an economic issue, but it's a bit of a stretch to see how it's an environmental concern, beyond its relationship to the negative environmental impacts of idling. Nonetheless, automobile service levels are an important part of environmental impact statement (EIS) analysis in nearly every state.

The current practice of drawing the system boundary for EISs at the project level has a perverse effect. It results in calculation methodologies that assume that every person who comes and goes from a project generates an additional car trip on neighboring streets. *Trip Generation: An ITE Informational Report,* the reference guide put out by the Institute of Transportation

Engineers, which governs these calculations for EIS purposes, has no standard framework for adjusting the ratio of car trips as a result of increased urban density, improved pedestrian connections, or mix of uses.[10] Developers who work on compact urban infill projects find that the burden of proof about car trip reductions ends up resting squarely in their court. If the system boundary were redrawn at the neighborhood level, where interconnectivity between uses and the feasibility of pedestrian and bicycle trips can be evaluated, higher-density projects would likely show a *reduction* in car trips in many cases, and at the very least a significant number of intraneighborhood pedestrian trips to offset the new interneighborhood car trips.

Redrawing the system boundary at the city or regional scale levels the playing field even further. At this scale complete neighborhoods or subareas of the city reduce highway miles traveled. Compact projects that add uses or create more access to an existing mix of uses actually *free up highway capacity*. Infill development projects would benefit in two ways from an environmental impact analysis that considered these broader system boundaries: First, the projects would not be required to bear as much additional cost for improvements to surrounding streets. Second, appeals and roadblocks to infill projects would be lessened, improving these projects' competitive feasibility relative to outlying greenfield projects. The same logic about trip generation could also be applied to parking adequacy analysis, which is another significant part of state environmental protection policies.

Revise state environmental protection policies to strike a balance among state, regional, and local interests.

States should revise environmental protection policies to prevent them from being used as tools against regional land use policies and density targets. Some recent Seattle area project challenges illustrate this rather well. Between 2007 and 2011, Touchstone Corporation, a Seattle developer, worked to entitle a project in Kirkland, Washington. Kirkland is a former shipbuilding town that became a bedroom community to Seattle when the shipbuilding industry declined after the Second World War and bridges were built to connect the east side of Lake Washington to Seattle. Several apartment and condo projects built through the 1980s and 1990s led to a significant downtown residential area. In 2001 the City of Kirkland released a strategic plan that specifically targeted an area immediately adjacent to the east of downtown called Parkplace for commercial growth. While Kirkland's downtown retail did well in the summer when the waterfront attracted visitors, it struggled in the winter. Further-more, many tech companies that were homegrown in Kirkland left the city as they grew because there were no large office spaces to accommodate them.

Touchstone proposed to redevelop Parkplace (an ailing strip mall surrounded by surface parking) into a more intense office-over-retail mixed-use project. The proposed project required a rezone because it essentially doubled the square footage of the old zoning on the site. The project was consistent with the city's comprehensive plan and benefited the neighborhood by putting all parking underground, restoring the street network through the twelve-acre site, and creating large public spaces at ground level and public rooftop terraces with views of the lake several blocks away. Despite winning an award for exceptional urban planning from a regional coalition of nonprofits, two opponents using SEPA delayed the project for four years. Although Touchstone persevered, this kind of legal power in the hands of even two opposed parties illustrates how SEPA can easily thwart urban redevelopment and why many developers are dissuaded from even attempting ambitious infill projects.

In another example, in 2007 Seattle Children's Hospital, an award-winning children's facility that serves five states in the Northwest region, was becoming overcrowded and needed to expand. The hospital purchased several adjacent buildings and sought authorization to redevelop these areas into additional facilities. The EIS that was part of the SEPA analysis showed that there would be additional traffic impacts that could not be mitigated by road widening at some of the adjacent intersections. This finding allowed some residents in the adjacent neighborhood of Laurelhurst to delay the project for nearly two years. Clearly, serving sick children at a location that is highly accessible from many points in the city is in the community interest, and one central facility is indisputably more efficient from a service (and an energy) point of view. Yet it's a prime example of how environmental protection policies can provide too many tools for opponents of infill to delay (and even halt) worthwhile projects.

Environmental Nonprofits and Private Sector Companies

Get involved in crafting policy and providing feedback about what works.

There is a lot of work to be done at the regulatory level, and this tends to scare private sector companies. But they have an important role to play. Regulatory agencies are good at increasing regulation but are generally not very focused on simplifying and eliminating it. The private sector understands how unhelpful more regulation can be in fostering adoption of new technologies and processes in a massive way; it has a key role to play in helping governments understand the barriers to a carbon-efficient economy. There is a great need at every level of government to hear from private enterprises that have internalized the problem of climate change and to get input on solutions that meet that challenge and also allow them to make money. This is not a project for the faint of heart or the shortsighted, but true engagement in solutions that limit greenhouse gas emissions and unleash market power are within reach if the private sector gets involved in the challenge of policy development.

Work in coalitions.
....

Two conditions will set the stage for the most effective solutions to evolve. First, the private sector needs to think broadly about the challenge. Transforming to a carbon-efficient economy will be complex and will require big-picture thinking about how to create customer value and delight: single-issue self-interest will not secure a productive seat at the policy table. Second, agents in the private, nonprofit, and public sectors need to create opportunities to collaborate with one another. Participants who work in broad coalitions bring more credibility about big-picture thinking, speak in a louder voice, and can send clearer signals to policy makers.

Since 2005, the Urban Land Institute (ULI) has sponsored events called "Reality Check" in eleven regions across the country. The events bring together people from all sectors: local and regional governments, port authorities, developers, large corporations, entrepreneurs, environmental think tanks, university researchers, housing advocacy groups, and social equity watchdogs for one day of collaborative visioning. Participants are assigned to tables in highly diverse groups of ten, and each group receives a large-scale map of the region and a bag of color-coded Lego blocks representing all of the people and jobs that will be added to the region in the next twenty to forty years. Each table works together to find spaces for the new growth on their map, with only one rule: you have to fit every block in. Participants then use yarn to lay out where the region will need to invest in transportation infrastructure or where open space and green infrastructure investment should go.

The amazing thing about the exercise is that when population growth is a given and people are required to take a regional perspective, there is almost always a high degree of convergence between all of the participants about how to allocate space to absorb growth. Furthermore, transportation choices, compact walkable development, and carbon efficiency are clear criteria for allocation that all stakeholders readily agree on. In Seattle participating organizations sought to capitalize on the convergence discovered at a Reality Check in 2008 by forming the Quality Growth Alliance (QGA), a coalition that works on research and policy development tools to advance these common goals. QGA includes:

» Futurewise, an organization dedicated to ensuring vibrant cities, which in the past had often worked at cross purposes with developers.
» The Washington State chapter of the Commercial Real Estate Association, commonly known by the acronym NAIOP.
» Forterra (formerly known as the Cascade Land Conservancy), an organization founded to preserve working and wilderness land.
» The Master Builders Association, the association for Washington State home builders.
» Enterprise, a group focused on housing and social equity.
» The Puget Sound Regional Council.
» The University of Washington College of Built Environments.

By speaking with a common voice, these groups garner more than just the sum of their seats at the table. They constitute a powerful framework for broad thinking and a strong voice for transformative change that can meet their diverse individual goals as well as common goals for limiting climate change. The group has identified a set of criteria for desirable mixed-use infill, which developers can use to help gain approval for new projects that reflect the QGA objectives.

When environmental governments, nonprofits, and for-profit companies work in coalitions, they spur each other to more comprehensive and congruent solutions. By identifying common goals and articulating them together, they make their voices louder and clearer to regulators. In 2010 the Puget Sound Regional Council, working with QGA, secured a five-million-dollar grant from the U.S. Department of Housing and Urban Development (HUD) for a regional program called Growing Transit Communities to do more integrated regional planning for growth and infrastructure. The grant, which was also evaluated on the federal side by the Department of Transportation and the Environmental Protection Agency (EPA), was for the maximum amount awarded to any region for this type of work.

REGULATION IN A NUTSHELL

Much of our existing regulatory environment stands in the way of achieving carbon efficiency because it is simply not aligned with this objective. Where we have established regulations to promote CO_2 reduction, they tend to be piecemeal, uncoordinated, inconsistently applied, and sometimes even counterproductive. As daunting as the task may be, we will not achieve real change in emissions without a reasonably coordinated overhaul of regulations at all levels of government—from utility governance at the federal level to state environmental protection processes to zoning at the municipal level.

CHAPTER 4

REDUCE

You know you have achieved perfection in design not when you have nothing more to add, but when you have nothing more to take away.

—ANTOINE DE ST. EXUPERY

R educe is all about making things smaller and using less. Applying the principle of "reduce" to the built environment can create benefits at multiple levels. Smaller spaces have less embodied carbon because they use fewer materials; they also have lower operational costs. Compact neighborhoods create access with fewer mobility challenges: you can get where you need go without supplementing your human power with other forms of energy. Smaller and more compact spaces also incent reuse (which is the focus of chapter 5) by encouraging a mix of uses in the same space in different times of day, different seasons, or different decades. Shared use of space, in turn, allows us to reduce the overall amount of space we need to build.

In the past several decades much of the work on reducing energy use from the built environment has focused on making spaces more energy efficient. Although these efforts have led to significant progress, energy use has unfortunately not declined. From 1970 to 2004 the average size of a new single-family detached house in the United States increased from fifteen hundred square feet to more than twenty-three hundred square feet.[1] During this same period U.S. residential energy use per capita has remained more or less flat because improvements in energy efficiency have been offset by larger homes, increased air-conditioning, and more appliances filling up the larger spaces.[2]

In recent years there have been signs that increases in average home sizes may be leveling off. Smaller new homes have begun to emerge in the wake of the 2008 economic crisis.[3] Statistics show that (usually smaller) homes in walkable communities are preserving their value or rising in value more quickly than their suburban counterparts.[4] An increasing majority of people state that they prefer smaller homes with shorter commutes over larger homes with a longer commutes.[5] Notwithstanding these trends, many Americans still simply don't want to live in compact townhouses; instead, they prefer single-family homes with yards.[6] This chapter explores strategies that can support a market transformation that uses fewer resources more efficiently, without reducing customer satisfaction.

RECOGNIZING OPPORTUNITIES TO USE LESS

Reducing the amount of space or materials we use does not have to mean that we move to a culture of scarcity. Smaller, simpler, and higher-quality mechanisms can generate delight for customers. The iPhone, the motorcycle, and sushi are all examples of products that combine small scale with an emphasis on craftsmanship and quality of the user experience to command market share or a price premium over some of their larger, bulkier counterparts.

At the same time that the size of houses has increased (and the number of inhabitants per home has decreased), the amount of space used per office worker has, if anything, decreased. In the 1970s large individual offices were the norm for many professionals. In 2009 the average space per worker at Microsoft (where the average income is well over a hundred thousand dollars) is less than two hundred square feet, and many companies currently allocate even less space per employee. Given the increase in job mobility over the same period, it's easy to argue that companies must now work harder to retain a talented workforce, but more office space is not how they do it. At Microsoft the most valued perks are excellent health care benefits, flexibility to work from home, generous parental leave, top-notch sports field and workout facilities, and company-sponsored transit service that brings employees from their neighborhoods around the region to the Redmond corporate campus. Clearly, there is a way to provide more value while using less space.

In contrast to our growing dwellings, tiny "microhomes" have generated significant attention from both the design and sustainability communities. Tumbleweed Tiny House Company is one firm that has found just such a niche. Founded by Jay Shafer in 1997, Tumbleweed, based in Sebastopol, California, distributes its signature small, impeccably crafted, detached homes all over the United States and sells plans for small homes to clients around the world. How small? Tumbleweed's smallest code-compliant single-family home is 251 square feet, designed for a one- to two-person household.[7] They're not for everybody, but the surge in demand for these home plans over the past few years has shown that it is possible to make a small, well-crafted architectural product that appeals to the market. Microhome owners will pay more than $200 per square foot for some of the more upscale models, compared with the average home price of about $120 per square foot in most parts of the United States.[8]

A more mundane but also more widespread example of "using less" is milk packaging. In eastern Canada, Israel, and in parts of Europe, South America, and Africa, milk is sold in plastic bags.[9] Everyone has a container at home that holds the bag upright in the refrigerator like the one in the upper part of figure 4.1. To open the bag, you simply snip off a corner and pour. In the United States, if you buy more than a quart of milk, it's sold in a gallon jug like the one in the lower part of the figure. The jug is more expensive to produce than the bags, less efficient from a wholesale packaging point of view, less efficient to transport, and creates a lot more garbage, or uses more energy to recycle, and it uses more fossil fuels in the raw materials. This is one of those baffling things that's "just the way we do it." You could make the argument that people in the United States don't have the little holder with the handle at home, but you could provide that *for free* for about same cost as one milk jug. If milk distributors gave everyone a free bag holder and then sold milk in bags, they would reduce unit costs, use fewer hydrocarbons, create less waste, *and their customers probably wouldn't care.* Frankly,

4.1. Milk in a plastic bag and milk in a disposable jug. Photos by Keir Dahlke and A-P Hurd

it's amazing it hasn't happened already. The point of this, of course, is that there is still room for private enterprise to do things that reduce greenhouse gas emissions and that are fundamentally aligned with their profit interest.

HOW WE CAN USE LESS

STRATEGY #4: Focus not only on energy efficiency (energy per square foot) but also on the denominator: find ways to create more value while consuming fewer resources. Reducing is about using less to meet people's real needs just as well, or better.

Federal Government

The carbon and water taxes described in chapter 2 are the best tools to encourage consumers to reconsider the amount of space, embodied energy, and operational energy they use. However, with these price signals in place, there are several other strategies that can also be employed.

Support the development of location-efficient mortgages.

Through its mortgage agencies such as the Federal National Mortgage Association (FNMA, or Fannie Mae) and the Federal Home Loan Mortgage Corporation (FHLMC, or Freddie Mac) the federal government can encourage location-efficient mortgages. When people are being qualified for mortgages, banks use a few rules of thumb to decide if the applicants can pay off the loan. A common one of these is that the monthly mortgage payment should not be more than 30 percent of the applicant's monthly take-home income. This assumes that the rest of their income goes to things like food and transportation. Over the past several years, as more people entered the housing market, a phenomenon emerged that has been colloquially referred to as "drive till you qualify." People were willing to pay more in automobile costs to find a home where the mortgage payment was below the 30 percent threshold. Unfortunately, automobile costs (and gas prices in particular) are the most volatile part of their budgets. When gas prices rose over the past decade, particularly in 2007, it brought on a rash of foreclosures. Research led by Scott Bernstein, president of the Chicago-based Center for Neighborhood Technology (CNT), has shown that the rate of foreclosures in cities like Chicago and Los Angeles increased most dramatically in neighborhoods that had long single-occupancy vehicle (SOV) commutes and little access to public transit.[10]

Location-efficient mortgages begin to offer a solution to this problem because they consider the total of transportation and housing costs in making a decision about whether an applicant qualifies for a mortgage. In a reasonable location-efficient mortgage model, transportation and mortgage costs must be below 60 to 65 percent of an applicant's take-home pay. While mortgage holders are still subject to price volatility in fuel costs, the alternate formula reduces the incentive to crank up the driving cost to get the mortgage payment down. In fact, CNT has shown that in areas well served by transit, car ownership per household can decrease from two or three vehicles to one or even to zero. Eliminating one vehicle allows prospective buyers to afford about six thousand to eight thousand dollars more in mortgage payments per year, and makes them less subject to fuel price volatility, while still preserving the same free cash flow for other uses.[11]

Location-efficient mortgages can reduce automobile use as well as road and other infrastructure costs while increasing consumer satisfaction. They fit into the category of enabling economic frameworks that increase economic efficiency discussed in chapter 2. Unfortunately, although these mortgages underwent pilot testing in four U.S. metropolitan markets (Chicago, Seattle, the San Francisco Bay, and Los Angeles County), they are not currently available in the United States.[12]

Avoid subsidies that effectively prevent local agriculture.

Another area where the federal government can reduce water and energy consumption is in the area of agriculture. While not traditionally considered to be part of the "built environment," local agriculture and urban agriculture are part of our land use pattern and have emerged as a way to reduce the transportation impact of getting food from where it's grown to where it is consumed. Consumer demand is increasing for locally produced foods, but traditional federal subsidies for agriculture not only result in high costs for taxpayers, they also create market distortions that stand in the way of local food supply chains. This in turn often makes locally produced food uncompetitive. The complex (and international) question of agricultural subsidies is beyond the scope of this book, but agriculture is ultimately a land use issue and needs to be considered as we develop carbon-efficient regional economies.

Local Governments

Revisit zoning and building code requirements that stand in the way of affordable and compact housing.

Local governments frequently have zoning in place that made sense historically but stands directly in the way of the type and density of neighborhoods that foster carbon-efficiency and that consumers increasingly desire. For example, as a group, apartment dwellers are excellent candidates to find value in living close-in. When you consider that apartment dwellers don't have backyards in the first place, and that they live in smaller spaces where the neighborhood and its public spaces *are* their backyards, it makes sense that they don't want to live in the distant suburbs in the same way that owners of single-family homes do.

However, one of the key challenges of increasing urban density is the lack of affordable and low-income rental housing. Affordable close-in apartments often face an uphill battle with condominiums in the competition for construction capital. Frequently, existing multifamily residential zoning does not allow smaller apartments to be built, so it is easier for investors to amortize the cost of the underlying land over condos rather than larger apartments that renters generally cannot afford. The logical question one might ask is, Why are smaller apartments not allowed? The answer is that many zoning and building codes were designed decades ago at a time when minimum size limits for multifamily units were judged to be important; these regulations remain in place today, preventing the development of small, efficient, well-built spaces that are reasonably priced.

If we try to travel even further down the reduction path with respect to housing, we find that many cities place virtually insurmountable obstacles in the way of buildings that are designed around the concept of shared facilities like kitchens and laundry. These prohibitions were often conceived in the bad old days of seedy boarding houses. Yet modern, high-quality incarnations of this type of dwelling have demonstrated that they can very successfully meet the needs of people like students, lower-income workers with long working hours, or individuals who are in transition or are focused on saving money.[13] Cities need to concentrate not on preventing this type of facility, but rather on how to make them successful, because they can maximize per capita carbon-efficiency, especially when they are close-in or near public transportation corridors.

Cities can also allow for creative opportunities for infill at higher densities without taking down existing buildings and while preserving the character of existing neighborhoods. Seattle, for example, recently increased zoning flexibility to allow for cottage housing developments. This permits the construction of secondary dwelling units on existing single-family lots, as long as the new unit is less than eight hundred square feet. Other ways to achieve this goal in an infill setting include reducing or even eliminating minimum lot sizes on single-family lots to allow for subdivision of lots and small unit infill.

Environmental Nonprofits and Private Sector Companies

Include operational and per capita considerations in the certification of sustainable buildings and neighborhoods.

One area where certifying bodies such as the U.S. Green Building Council (USGBC) can influence reduction of space and materials is in extending their certification programs to include operations; the USGBC's LEED standard has already taken steps in this direction with some of its operational programs.[14] A useful next step would be for those programs to cover patterns of use, including things like occupant density and shared uses through the day, week, month, or year. For instance, a school might pair some of its operations with a place of worship or a summer camp to meet this designation. In the case of LEED for housing, it would be useful to consider not just energy efficiency per square foot but also per occupant. In commercial buildings this metric could be adjusted to energy efficiency per occupant-hour. All of this would work to incent the design of highly versatile spaces, and once a building is complete, it would continue to encourage higher-intensity utilization of space.

Create market transparency around the operational energy performance of buildings.

Beyond certification systems, there are other ways in which reporting mechanisms can improve the market for smaller, more efficient buildings. As part of its National Strategy on Energy Efficiency, the Australian federal government in November of 2010 began requiring sellers of commercial buildings to disclose the energy performance of their buildings; in 2012 the requirement is being extended to home sellers as well.[15] A Washington State bill signed into law in 2009 requires nonresidential buildings to disclose their Energy Star ratings to prospective lessees or buyers starting in 2011. Similar measures to Washington's have been proposed in Ontario, Canada.[16] This is a step in the right direction because it gets data into the market and allows the market to respond. According to a December 2009 study by Jones Lang LaSalle's Australian office, corporate real estate executives factor energy efficiency heavily into their leasing and portfolio decisions.[17] LessEn (an initiative of the Urban Land Institute) has taken a step that promises to make energy consumption information even more readily available. It has developed an application for smartphones that allows users to instantly find the energy use in any building in the cities they cover.[18]

An even better solution than a government mandate, however, would be for listing systems, such as MLS and CoStar, to include measurement standards and data fields to report this information as a service to their customers. This would lower the transactional cost of getting the information to the market. Buildings that had low energy costs would want to post them, and inefficient buildings would be asked about their performance and could be motivated to improve. A key challenge of energy disclosure for commercial buildings is correcting for the energy intensiveness of the tenant's business. This is a place where private sector building owners and investors need to be engaged in the creation of metrics that reflect the intrinsic energy efficiency of their buildings. Investors love Microsoft's credit rating on a lease, but no one wants their building to look bad because it is filled with software developers compiling code on three desktops!

Transparency can also work at the individual level, gently encouraging individual residents and tenants to reduce energy consumption through changes in their behavior. The Toyota Prius, for example, features a dashboard "energy monitor" screen that reports the vehicle's gas mileage to the driver in real time. When drivers can see immediately how certain habits, like accelerating quickly or driving above the speed limit, drain their gas tanks, many of them become surprisingly focused on driving more fuel efficiently. Web sites have even sprung up offering tips: "Unlock the mysteries of the 'pulse and glide' technique—and other toe-wiggling strategies for pushing Prius miles per gallon to the edge."[19] Using the same principle, easy-to-read energy meters located in a visible place inside homes or offices can show exactly which appliances are using the most energy, and at what times, allowing occupants to react and have the immediate satisfaction of seeing the numbers respond.

Developers

Promote life-cycle cost analysis on owner-occupied and build-to-suit buildings.

Developers undertake buildings with a variety of risk profiles. Owner-occupied buildings present the lowest risk because the owner plans to maintain ownership of the building for a long time. Developers of these buildings can implement strategies that have a longer-term payback or that might not be as highly valued by other users. Furthermore, owner-occupiers tend to view buildings as a crucible where their primary productive business takes place. They are willing to consider—and value—building strategies that fundamentally enhance the productivity of their employees.

In the next tier are build-to-suit developments. These projects are typically developed with specific long-term tenants in mind. The tenants pre-lease the building, so the developer has an identified customer as it designs and builds the building. Pre-leased, build-to-suit buildings are riskier than owner-occupied buildings for a few reasons: the tenant can go out of business, requiring the developer to re-lease to another tenant; the tenant's lease is typically ten to twenty years, so the building will need to be re-tenanted at some point; and lastly, the developer may want to sell the building, so versatility is also of value to the subsequent owner. Build-to-suit developers are typically willing to take some innovation risk, but less so than the owner-developers.

Finally there are speculative developments. In this case, the tenants have not yet been identified, so the builder tries to develop a building that will be appealing to the greatest number of potential tenants. Versatility, low upfront cost, and market standardization are much more important than innovation.

The point of this discussion is that it's important to recognize that in some situations developers are better positioned to do things differently, because they have less risk, and more to gain from trying out new strategies or technologies. In owner-occupied or build-to-suit buildings, life-cycle cost analysis is increasingly being used throughout the design process to evaluate new strategies. Life-cycle cost analysis is a method of comparing the total costs—including initial, operating, maintenance, and replacement costs (and sometimes less tangible costs, such as program flexibility and employee productivity)—of various alternatives, on a present-value basis so that the costs one system saves over time can be compared to the initial capital savings of another. This framework provides the opportunity for developers with lower market risk to look at some fundamentally innovative design decisions that are tied to the principle of "reduce."[20] For example, this type of analysis is leading some developers to eliminate communications cabling in favor of wireless infrastructure.

Looking at life-cycle costs and understanding user flexibility can also allow designers to look at new ways (or sometimes look again at old ways) of designing for peak conditions; this can lead to significant savings as well as greater energy efficiency. Some building owners in temperate climates, for instance, are eliminating cooling systems in favor of passive cooling strategies. In Seattle the design firm Weber Thompson created its new headquarters with a courtyard design and operable windows that optimize natural lighting and passive heating and cooling. The four-story, LEED-certified building, completed in 2008, was the first major office building in decades to be developed in Seattle without air-conditioning.[21]

Although this means that temperatures inside buildings shift more widely with the seasons, companies have found that eliminating HVAC costs is a cost-saving strategy, even when they consider the cost of sending their employees home early on the few hot summer days when the office gets uncomfortable. The HVAC system for most commercial office buildings typically represents about 30 percent of the construction cost and 20 to 45 percent of the net operating expense, so reducing this component can yield huge construction and operational savings. In a typical business, even if five days per employee are lost per year because of the lack of air-conditioning, the tenant still comes out ahead.[22] Along the same lines, but somewhat less aggressively, other developers are working with tenants to offer operable windows and widen the acceptable temperature range for the space. While this falls short of eliminating HVAC systems altogether, it does reduce the capacity and infrastructure required, making a smaller, less costly, and more carbon-efficient system an appropriate choice.

Include separate metering as part of standard tenant improvements, and let tenants pay for only the energy and water they use.

The way that many commercial buildings are delivered to the market reflects a limiting framework. *Cold, dark shell* is the term used to refer to commercial buildings that aren't built out yet with tenant improvements, such as lighting, carpeting, walls, and sometimes even the distribution portion of the ventilation system. The idea behind this is to allow maximum flexibility for later customization. When tenants sign a long-term lease in such a new building, they receive an allowance from the landlord to build out their space as they like.

When they invest in that build-out, tenants have the option to acquire high-efficiency components that will conserve energy and water, but rarely do they have an incentive to do so. Because single electrical and water meters are generally installed for the entire building, tenants are levied operational costs on a proportional basis to the ratio of the building they occupy. This disincents water- and energy-saving investments as part of the tenant space build-outs and provides no encouragement for conservation behaviors among the tenants' employees because such behaviors have no direct impact on their utility costs. There is no real reason—again other than tradition—that developers can't include these simple meters as part of the tenant improvement budget and require them to be installed throughout the building floor by floor or on a portion of a floor as part of the build-out. Tenants, for their part, stand to gain by being responsible only for the energy and water that they consume, and not for the excesses of their neighbors.

REDUCE IN A NUTSHELL

One of the most effective ways to reduce our carbon footprint is to reduce the amount of built space we use and make the usage patterns for our buildings more energy efficient. A focus on increasing the availability of attractive compact homes that reduce commute times would be a very important step in this direction. Increasing the transparency of operating costs for buildings (where energy is a dominant factor) would also go a long way to encourage energy-conserving buildings and practices.

BUILT TO LAST

I only feel angry when I see waste. When I see people throwing away things we could use.

—MOTHER TERESA

I
n the world of consumer products, "reduce, reuse, recycle" is the catchphrase for strategies that reduce waste. When talking about the built environment, it is more relevant to think of these in two separate categories—the first being "reduce," which is discussed in chapter 4, and the second, "reuse, restore, retrofit," which is the subject of this chapter. *Restore* and *retrofit* are the built environment equivalents of *recycle*, a strategy that has considerable potential for carbon-efficiency when applied to buildings and neighborhoods.

Our decision to leave out *recycle* as it applies to materials and subsystems is a deliberate one. While recycling reduces landfill waste and, in some cases, reduces the energy needed to produce new materials, recycling of building materials is generally very energy and labor intensive. This is not exclusively a built-environment problem. The increasing prevalence (and perceived virtue) of recycling over the past several years has overshadowed awareness that significant energy is often required in the process. Recycling a plastic water bottle is probably better than sending it to a landfill but certainly not as beneficial as using a reusable bottle or cup. For some materials in some places, maintaining the best environmental balance (accounting for landfill and energy use) actually means shifting away from recycling.

About five years ago the City of Amsterdam—an early leader in recycling—abolished its curbside garbage and organic waste pick-up in most parts of the city. The city's rigorous analysis showed that picking up these items was much more energy intensive than they had realized. They also found that when people perceive recycling as a positive behavior, they tend to generate more waste overall. In Amsterdam today citizens can only recycle their larger plastics, and only by returning them to the point of purchase for a refund of deposit. Cans are not recycled at all, and perhaps as a result of this, cans are not very heavily used. Amsterdam residents can still recycle glass and paper by bringing them to the very conveniently located garbage and recycling drop-off points.

In contrast with recycling, reuse consumes much less energy because products are not entirely reprocessed. Reuse of products like refillable glass beer bottles is quite resource and cost efficient but only really works when products and equipment are highly standardized, and when the means of compliance are widely understood and practiced among both producers and consumers. In the built environment, where projects are usually created one at a time over a number of years by many different teams of people, these characteristics are generally not present. It takes more design ingenuity and responsiveness to incorporate old materials or systems, such as brick walls, beams, or other infrastructure into new or retrofit projects. Clearly, a design process that identifies opportunities for reuse upfront and not as an afterthought will be far more successful in facilitating reuse.

Restore and retrofit are concepts that apply more to entire buildings. Since the 1960s, the United States has shifted from a manufacturing-driven economy to a service-based one. Manufacturing and product supply chains that remain competitive have dramatically reduced inventory levels. In the service sectors space per worker has generally decreased, as discussed in chapter 4. As a result, a large stock of old office and industrial buildings and even neighborhoods have become obsolete. These buildings contain a huge amount of embodied energy, are often expensive to tear down, and generate a lot of landfill waste when they are demolished. Unfortunately, few old buildings are successfully restored and returned to use. If we could find ways to galvanize the ingenuity of the real estate industry and the construction supply chain to create new life for old buildings, it could potentially generate tremendous economic returns. In this chapter we'll look at some of the ways to get there.

"Built to last," our chapter title, is about doing it once and doing it right, so that your product will have value for a long time. Whether you drive a fifteen-year-old Honda Accord, wear your grandfather's watch, or still use the same toboggan as when you were a child, you know that well-made things last longer. Quality is really just the corollary to reuse.

RECOGNIZING QUALITY

The garment industry employs many strategies to reuse or retrofit clothing until all the value has been extracted from it. When an item of clothing is no longer required, most people in North America look for an organization such as Goodwill Industries that will find another use for it. When clothes do not meet the standard for resale in the United States, they are often sold to salvage brokers that ship and resell them internationally (generally in developing nations) or to textile recyclers that turn them into industrial rags or fibers to make products like new carpet.[1]

Another reuse channel for clothing is provided by the consignment store industry, which sells higher-end used clothing and is a thriving (and growing) business in most cities in North America. Garments can also be tailored down, and even made into other items. Independent fashion designers in many cities have brought high-style cachet to reused clothing by making new garments out of interesting pieces of old ones. Secondhand clothing usually costs less than new quality fabrics, and it often takes less energy to stitch finished components together than to pattern and construct new clothing from scratch. These clothes appeal to customers because of their inventiveness and the glimpse they afford into the history of the original garments.

This view into a history of previous uses can be aesthetically appealing in buildings as well. In Toronto the site of the former Gooderham and Worts Distillery, the largest collection of Victorian-era industrial architecture in North America, has been preserved by owner Cityscape Holdings Inc. The historic Distillery District is a vibrant and pedestrian-oriented community of residences, visual and performing arts spaces, and independent retailers (depicted in figure 5.1).[2] In the United States the Rose Smart Growth Investment Fund applies energy-saving retrofits to historic buildings in transit-supported urban areas across the country, adding value while preserving the structures' unique character (one of the fund's first projects is shown in figure 5.1).[3] In the United Kingdom a firm called Urban Space Management has taken a modular approach to reuse. Its Container City concept is a model for stacking and linking old shipping containers in various configurations to create artful, appealing commercial and residential spaces (as shown in figure 5.1).[4] Urban Space Management has now completed sixteen projects using

5.1. Reuse in Toronto's Distillery District, London's Container City, and Seattle's Joseph Vance Building. Photos by Sue Wilson, Julia Levitt, and A-P Hurd

its technique, which has an added "reuse" aspect: a "container city" can be quickly disassembled and reused elsewhere if the land it is on is required for another use.[5]

The Gooderham and Worts example—as a collection of buildings—highlights some of the key ingredients to successful neighborhood-level reuse. First, the technical and budget risk challenges of reuse are often compensated for by the rich grain of a neighborhood that can command premium rents. Conversely, the owner of a single building may not benefit from taking on the challenges of reuse if the rest of the neighborhood is redeveloped without regard to preserving character. As a result, successful examples of building reuse are often really examples of neighborhood reuse with either one master developer (as at Gooderham and Worts) or a group of developers that has established a sense of cooperation and trust. In the Pike-Pine corridor in Seattle, for example, it is the relationships between developers and landowners in the neighborhood that have led to a mode of redevelopment that has substantial emphasis on reuse along with preservation of (and contribution to) the neighborhood character.

Not all old buildings are alike, and not all parts of them can be successfully deconstructed and readapted or reused. This creates significant risk for developers who contemplate reusing the shell or other portions of buildings. Often, the feasibility of reuse is difficult to determine as part of a noninvasive due-diligence process. The resulting budget contingencies make projects uneconomic. Plaster, drywall, asbestos-contaminated structures, and composite roof shingles are all notoriously difficult to reuse or even to extract as part of a remodel. Clearly, the best way to handle these types of reuse challenges is to avoid designing them into our buildings in the first place. In the consumer product world, where life cycles are shorter than those of the built environment, many manufacturing designers have been thinking seriously since the 1990s about design for reuse. This is also known as design for maintenance, design for deconstructability, or design for disposal, and it is part of a life-cycle approach to product design.

When systems are designed with standard modular parts, this principle argues, those parts can be replaced if they fail, rather than throwing out the whole system. Water faucets are an everyday example: they tend to be made mostly of metal but they usually have rubber or plastic washers inside them that maintain the watertight seal when the taps are turned on or off. These components are designed to be the only part of the faucet that wears out. Faucets are made in a way such that anyone with a screwdriver and a small wrench can easily repair them using a standard low-cost washer from the hardware store.

Unfortunately, reuse doesn't happen as much as it could because many products are not made to allow their components to be repaired or replaced.

In addition to design for reuse, exchanges for used products are critical to getting them back into service. Craigslist has become a household name in most metropolitan areas in the United States, catalyzing reuse as an everyday option. Habitat for Humanity operates hundreds of outlets in the United States and Canada (called The ReStore) that contain everything from old doors to used sinks to old fir floorboards from school gymnasia. The ReStore business model creates value from used building materials otherwise headed for landfills, and Habitat for Humanity uses the proceeds to build affordable housing.[6]

A very successful larger-scale example of design for reuse in the built environment can be found in the evolution of office systems over the past fifty years. Before about 1960, nearly all white-collar office work took place either in fixed-wall offices or in open areas with no privacy at all. The subsequent widespread adoption of moveable privacy panels and modular furniture, even at the highest executive levels in many companies, has saved untold amounts of materials and energy. Perhaps most important, this dramatic change in the office framework was economically motivated. It has led to huge financial savings for businesses and governments, and improved flexibility by allowing rapid office reconfiguration to meet changing business conditions.

Because of long building life cycles, this approach has been slow to catch on at the building level, but reuse is gaining significant attention as a strategy in recent years. The U.S. Green Building Council's (USGBC) Greenbuild conference has focused increasing attention on reuse through panels that address both the technical and regulatory challenges. For instance, on the technical side, materials like metal panels and solid wood elements (for cladding or interiors) are relatively easy to incorporate, and they offer the potential for reuse again at a later date. Metal panels also have a very positive energy balance if they do end up being recycled. In 2007 a team of designers from HyBrid and Owen Richards Architects in Seattle designed and developed an energy-efficient single-family home that can be built for less than a hundred thousand dollars. The design, which won the $99K House Competition sponsored by Rice Design Alliance and the American Institute of Architects Houston Chapter, is organized around the principle of reuse. Demountable and moveable wall systems offer built-in flexibility, allowing residents to divide the home into various configurations, or even into two separate dwelling units, as their needs change over time.[7]

This is a good example of designing for reuse because reconfiguration produces an outcome similar to remodeling but creates almost no waste. These stories illustrate the preconditions for successful reuse or retrofit: simple deconstructable design, a marketplace, and a flexible customer. So how do we put these elements in place to enable greater reuse, restoration, and retrofit of the built environment?

HOW WE CAN BUILD TO LAST

STRATEGY #5: Create a reuse and restoration culture by focusing on designing for enduring quality and flexibility. Nurture marketplaces for reuse and quickly fix aspects of the regulatory environment that discourage reuse.

Federal Government

Focus Department of Housing and Urban Development (HUD) funding on creating long-term life-cycle value in high-quality housing and neighborhoods.

The federal government through HUD influences many decisions about housing quality. Quality and longevity aspirations are always in tension with the desire to create more housing for more people. It is helpful to think about quality in terms of aggregate spending over fifty years versus aggregate utility (customer value) over the same period. Some aspects of quality (such as finishes) may be less important, while the ability to restore, to replace parts, and to keep existing buildings looking good has more enduring value. If buildings can also be designed to support flexible uses, this contributes to their longevity as well.

Why is flexible, high-quality housing important? It's helpful to think for a minute of the system dynamics that drive economic value. When a high-quality building is developed, its initial cost may be more than that of a less well-built structure, but if it continues to look good over time, people are far more likely to keep taking care of it. On the other hand, deterioration fosters lack of pride, and lack of pride combined with disrepair often fosters graffiti and vandalism. Disrepair and lack of flexibility in buildings increase population mobility, which reduces community strength and pride. When neighborhoods lose their vitality and pride, they are on a loss-of-value trajectory that is nearly impossible to halt. Not only do the buildings suffer, but the loss goes even deeper, undermining the value of the land. Buildings that are dilapidated suffer structurally, making them some of the most difficult candidates for reuse or retrofit.

Investing upfront in quality and flexibility increases the first life of buildings as well as their retrofit potential. Architect Michael Pyatok, nationally recognized for his award-winning designs of affordable housing, has championed investment in high-quality, well-designed buildings in part because of their staying power; he observes that when well-designed buildings are in need of repair, communities support them instead of arguing to tear them down.[8] HUD and the Department of Energy (DOE) currently operate several programs that encourage and support the retrofitting and preservation of existing affordable housing. To the extent that HUD can foster flexible high-quality neighborhoods that keep looking good, it will drive more value across all human and environmental metrics.

Enable municipalities to finance energy retrofits to existing buildings and pay back loans through property tax assessments.

Over the past few years Boulder, Colorado, and Berkeley, California, have begun to finance property-level energy-efficiency improvements using a tool called PACE (property assessed clean energy). Several other states have enabled similar programs. PACE allows municipalities to provide capital to building owners and homeowners for energy-efficiency renovations and to collect payments on the amortizing obligation as part of the property tax bill. This mechanism creates access to funding with long-term amortizations (consistent with energy-saving investment payback periods) that are otherwise difficult to obtain.[9]

In 2010 the Federal Housing Financing Agency (FHFA) significantly curbed PACE when it directed Fannie Mae and Freddy Mac to stop underwriting mortgages with PACE financing. In its news release, FHFA cited the following reason for withholding its support: "[Liens associated with PACE financing] present significant risk to lenders and secondary market entities, may alter valuations for mortgage-backed securities and are not essential for successful programs to spur energy conservation." The press release added: "While the first lien position offered in most PACE programs minimizes credit risk for investors funding the programs, it alters traditional lending priorities."[10]

As coauthors Jonathan Wilson, Maura Marcheski, and Elias Hinckley discuss in their article "The Great PACE Controversy," the financing concerns of FHFA and other stakeholders are legitimate (notwithstanding FHFA's gratuitous comment about whether PACE-like vehicles are necessary to promote energy conservation), but this has been a major setback for the residential energy retrofit market.[11] There are solutions to the challenges that PACE financing initially encountered, and we would urge everyone involved to recognize that these efforts were just a first try. The second and third efforts that are now under way should be pursued vigorously. A rationalized PACE program has the potential to provide a win for all stakeholders through long-term opportunities for owners to make energy-saving investments that future-proof buildings; municipalities to increase tax bases; and lenders and capital markets to put funds to work and develop new sources of potentially strong returns in the current low-yield environment.[12]

State Governments

Provide adequate liability protection to developers who want to clean up and redevelop contaminated infill sites.

State policy and staffing limitations create barriers to reuse of buildings and land. Infill sites are often contaminated to some degree, because environmental regulations have not always been as stringent as they are today. Dry cleaning fluid, oil, and other chemicals left behind in the soil are all-too-frequent challenges for urban projects. In many states environmental law holds the current owner responsible for site contamination, regardless of whether he or she contributed to the problem. Heavily contaminated sites are often owned by entities that do not have the means to clean them up. Potential buyers who would like to redevelop face large hurdles in limiting their liability before they close on a site. Even the characterization of the contamination (measuring and documenting the type and extent of it) on the site—to assess the problem—can create a liability if a test boring allows contaminants to leach to another layer of soil.

In many parts of the United States the characterization and clean-up process is administered at the state level. Typically the state agency brokers the clean-up plan with all the parties involved (including the original contaminators), approves the remediation plan, and monitors the result. In many states just getting a state project manager assigned to a site can take months, sometimes even up to two years. Creating and implementing the clean-up plan can take two years more. For urban sites with high land cost and high carrying cost, this wait is expensive and deters many developers from ever undertaking projects on potentially contaminated urban sites.

In a perfect world all sites would be perfectly cleaned up. In reality, the quest for a perfect solution to a difficult-to-quantify problem leaves many sites permanently contaminated. Sites that are too onerous for developers to clean up continue to leach pollutants into adjacent soil and groundwater for many more years, while developers turn their attention to more easily used green spaces instead. States could encourage developers to go ahead with infill projects that have site or building contamination by:

» Staffing oversight departments adequately so that private sector dollars can quickly get to work on the problem.
» Increasing fees to support faster processing and more predictable timeframes.
» Increasing liability protection for owners who inherit environmental problems by limiting the overall liability for noncontaminating land owners who work toward remediation.

Local Governments

Provide exchange facilities that encourage building material reuse.

....

Where local governments charge more for using the landfill, they create an incentive to deconstruct and set aside reusable materials. Local governments can also impact building material reuse by providing space at landfill sites for deconstructed materials to be warehoused and resold. The award-winning Monterey Regional Waste Management District in California's Monterey Peninsula operates its own reuse store, called the Last Chance Mercantile. The store is located near the local sanitary landfill and sells not only lumber and construction materials, but also used sporting goods, furniture, mulch, and other household items at affordable prices.[13] Providing convenient places in the city (perhaps adjacent to a new building materials store) to purchase salvaged materials further increases the efficiency of the market for salvaged building parts.

Create permitting structures that give developers time to deconstruct without additional carrying cost penalties.

....

One of the challenges of deconstructing buildings is that it takes more time than wholesale demolition. In the past few years some cities have created a streamlined permitting process whereby landowners can get a permit for deconstruction with less lead time than it takes to get approval for a demolition. The town of Los Altos Hills, California, takes the streamlining incentive a step further, waiving demolition permitting fees entirely for projects that will be deconstructed for later reuse.[14] Cities often justify these types of initiatives on the basis that they benefit from the reduction in landfill waste. If the property owner can begin deconstruction earlier, the cost of deconstruction goes down because the longer deconstruction process does not impact the cycle time of rebuilding. In effect, the developer's cost of carry on the property is not increased by the deconstruction process.

Lower barriers to historical preservation so that older buildings can be economically reused or integrated into higher-density development.

....

Historical preservation is another area where additional nuance could lead to reuse of more buildings and building parts. Preservation of historical buildings as cultural artifacts is important to the fabric and character of a city. However, this objective must be weighed against the need to keep buildings occupied and in good repair, as well as with judicious use of close-in land. Historical preservation, when taken to the extreme, preserves buildings that are derelict and can prevent deconstruction and reuse so completely that the buildings lose their value. When buildings lose their ability to attract capital, they fall into disrepair, are unoccupied, and lead to urban decay.

The challenge is to find a balance between perfect preservation and the scope of preservation to which it is possible to rally money and energy. Retention of facades and reuse of unique interior features, coupled with stronger economic incentives for restoration and retrofits, may be better tools to preserve a greater number of historical urban buildings. Examples of workable incentives are such things as zoning codes that offer developers additional development rights when they preserve a qualifying existing structure or even programs that allow owners of historical buildings to sell their development rights, allowing them to monetize the preservation of the original structure.

The nonprofit National Trust for Historic Preservation put its full weight behind preservation as a strategy for sustainability with the launch of its Preservation Green Lab in 2009. The Green Lab partners with cities and states to develop policies that integrate building preservation and reuse and the retrofitting of historical character neighborhoods as part of their broader climate change action plans. One of the Green Lab's most recent efforts has been an attempt to encourage innovative approaches to improving the energy performance of existing buildings. Currently, energy codes often prescribe the application of specific measures without recognizing the individual strengths and challenges of each existing building, without allowing for experimentation or innovation, and perhaps more disturbing, without requiring follow-up to determine whether the upgrades actually improved building energy performance. The lab has proposed an outcome-based energy code policy that would allow historical preservation and existing building rehab projects to use any appropriate means to achieve an agreed-upon energy target, as long as follow-up studies of building energy use show that the target is being met. The Green Lab is now partnering with the City of Seattle and the New Building Institute to pilot a national model for this outcome-based standard. The lab is also working with national partners on solutions for integrating new district energy systems into existing neighborhoods to dramatically improve their energy performance.

Integrate building codes to reduce discrepancies between building types.

As zoning codes evolved in the mid-twentieth century to specify different building types in different areas, building codes became more detailed and more specific to building types. Clearly, there is some variety in the standard specifications for different building types, but in general the broad segregation of building types within building codes tends to work against building reuse. For instance, hotel and residential codes have become so severely bifurcated that not only is reuse impacted, but it is also difficult to build the variety of smaller apartments that some customers would like. Ultimately isn't a hotel room just a very short-term apartment rental? The same principle is true between office and retail uses: if we could create just a bit more flexibility and commonality, it would ease the transition of ground floors back and forth between office uses and retail uses as neighborhoods evolve.

Environmental Nonprofits, Private Companies, and Developers

Consider the CO_2 impact of reuse in refining LEED and the Living Building Challenge.

....

The USGBC's LEED for New Construction (NC) program (first released in 1998) made an early move in the right direction by allocating points for building and material reuse.[15] In 2004, LEED for existing buildings (LEED-EB) was made available, providing another important step forward by helping the market understand sustainability in retrofitted and restored buildings.[16] However, there is not yet a clear emergent standard for measuring building or material reuse in construction projects. In recent years both nonprofit organizations and private companies have worked to advance the understanding of exactly how much embodied carbon comes with each material and each step of the process, but the information and methods for evaluation can be complex. To get it right, the calculation should probably take into account not only the material itself, but also where it came from and how it was transported to the site, its operating specifics, and often even specific details unique to the project site or region. A calculation methodology is dearly needed so that markets can quantify and value embodied emissions.

Create market transparency about embodied carbon.

....

The effort to develop an embodied-carbon methodology is a challenge worth embracing because, as in the case of operational emissions, once there is a standard for measurement, companies can use it to make decisions. For new construction, a carbon tax as described in chapter 2 would embed information about embodied carbon in the price of a building or the rent that is charged by the owner to generate an adequate profit. Incorporating embodied emissions into publically available information about the building on MLS and CoStar would provide additional transparency.

Continue to develop energy services, performance contracting, and financing mechanisms.

....

In chapter 1 we described how energy retrofit performance contracting is being used by educational institutions to improve the energy efficiency in schools. This is an excellent example of how the market can respond to enhance the value of old buildings and distribute that value across the supply chain in the form of economic opportunities for contractors and small businesses.

In its early years the energy service retrofit (ESCO) market has been primarily led by companies that are vertically integrated: they do the building analysis upfront, they provide financing, and they do the work. This is convenient for building owners but can have some negative side effects, including limits to project size and payback period, and even potential conflicts of interest. The retrofit provider may focus on the improvements that are most profitable for their contracting group, rather than the ones that have the biggest energy impact—particularly if their construction revenue is larger than their financing revenue. One solution to this is to disaggregate ESCO services; there is no reason that the people who do the work also need to finance it. The PACE example in the federal government section above is one way to do this, but private sector lenders could also create tools to evaluate these types of loans.

While energy retrofit loans may have long payback periods, the likelihood that the energy savings will occur is very high. Some lenders are even experimenting with energy retrofit loans that have a primary lien on the energy cost savings. By avoiding subordination to the mortgage (which is the first lien on the property), these new types of loans avoid property market risk and focus only on energy payback risk (which tends to be very low). Such creative structures emerging from the private sector have the potential to make a significant dent in providing low-cost funding for energy retrofits and making the ESCO market more competitive and efficient.

Consider life-cycle costs and build in elements that can be reused or that offer program flexibility.

Owner-developers who look at life-cycle costs over a longer term are increasingly finding value in modular, demountable systems for full walls, ceilings, and floors. For instance, raised floors where the space under the floor is a large air plenum are not justifiable on energy cost savings alone over short-term use. However, if the owner assumes even one reconfiguration of the space over the building life, the ability to move floor tiles to reposition air diffusers—rather than rip out substantial portions of an overhead air-distribution system—is so significant that under-floor air begins to make sense.

More generally, however, the whole approach to building life-cycle costing employed by nearly all developers and investors does not maximize investment in long-term quality. Currently an investment in a building that has a payback beyond forty years is not considered viable. At the same time, most investors would consider it foolhardy to acquire a ground lease of fewer than seventy-five years for a new building. Something is amiss here. The construction life-cycle cost analysis framework assumes the building will last only forty years, but the lease investment is governed by the assumption that it will exist for at least seventy-five years. It is our point of view that for most types of buildings, the seventy-five-year-plus horizon is more realistic, and life-cycle costing should be adjusted to reflect this reality. This would entail a change from the traditional "discounted cash flow" analysis model to one based on a more realistic long-term view of asset value. This perspective would likely lead to greater investment in long-term quality that would, in turn, foster reuse.

There may also be opportunities to use materials that are easier to reuse or recycle when user needs change, technologies change, or their useful life in the building is complete. Metal roofs on houses, for instance, which generally last fifty years, create lower capital replacement costs and lower landfill burden than do composite roofs, which last only about fifteen to twenty years. For many developers or even homeowners, however, this consideration is weakened by the relatively cheap costs of disposal compared with the higher up-front costs of the metal roof. If the costs of landfill disposal and energy increase over time, an old metal roof will be an asset to a house, whereas an old composite roof will be a liability. Finally, some elements of building design, such as high ceilings and opportunities for large window openings in the first story, provide the most flexibility of use (office, retail, residential, institutional) and create more options for reuse as a neighborhood evolves.

REUSE IN A NUTSHELL

The built environment contains a huge amount of embodied carbon, and new construction generates large volumes of additional CO_2. Unfortunately our buildings have not, by and large, been designed for reuse, and current economics drive us to fill our landfills with demolished older buildings and build new ones. We can make significant and lasting reductions in waste and CO_2 generation through a focus on creating enduring quality in buildings, by designing building subsystems for reuse, and by implementing practical measures that make it easier and more economically viable to reuse old buildings and materials.

CHAPTER 6

GREAT NEIGHBORHOODS

Don't buy the house, buy the neighborhood.

—RUSSIAN PROVERB

We know that there are patterns of development that make people feel good. We also know that certain patterns of development lead to lowered vehicle miles traveled. If we emphasize the second but ignore the first, we will never get compact patterns of land use that are actually desirable, profitable for developers to build, and carbon efficient all at the same time. Getting neighborhoods right is important for a number of reasons. First, neighborhoods are where people consistently find identity, belonging, and community. When these human needs are met, people's satisfaction with their living environment increases, and their inclination to transience declines. Second, neighborhoods are where people experience the built environment on foot and on bicycles, at speeds that allow them to notice the details of their surroundings. Third, neighborhoods are the scale at which access—to people, activities, goods, and services—can happen unencumbered by the barriers of distance and time. Complete and connected neighborhoods are time-efficient and satisfying places to live.

The current reality of disconnected, incomplete neighborhoods is a relatively recent phenomenon. In earlier times the village was the scale of human interaction and access. Because walking was the dominant form of transportation and long-distance trade was minimal, villages were, of necessity, self-sufficient with respect to food, products, and services. Many contemporary parents and children are fascinated when reading books such as Laura Ingalls Wilder's *Little House in the Big Woods* by the self-sufficiency of homesteader families in the late nineteenth century, who made almost everything they used. It's quite the opposite in today's cities and global trade environment, where every person and region is specialized and where access seems to almost always require long-distance, vehicular mobility. We can choose from a dozen varieties of sausage in the supermarket butcher case, but hardly anybody knows how to make sausage anymore.

The amazing global access we now enjoy is made possible by advances in technology and transportation. Getting groceries doesn't require the thirteen-hour, horse-drawn journey that Wilder's father made, but today's mobility is still expensive, not to mention carbon-intensive. It's both costly and inefficient to move yourself around to all the things you need if you are moving a four-thousand-pound SUV along with you. There's no question that most people are very happy that they no longer need to sew their own clothing, cure their own meats, and make soap from scratch. But still, there should be a way to get the things we need without spending hours in the car each day. Because we consume most of our goods at home, wouldn't it be better if they were generated near us when feasible, and if they came directly to us, resulting in the same amount of travel for the goods and zero travel for us? The solution to this is in the paradigm of neighborhood focus. Building complete neighborhoods is about more than community; it's also about access and shortening supply chains.

RECOGNIZING GREAT NEIGHBORHOODS

If we think about what we need to access in a typical day, we come up with a list something like this: our workplace, a cup of coffee, some help installing new tires, some exercise, a visit to the doctor, food for dinner, friends to eat dinner with. If our lives are organized at a neighborhood level and our neighborhood is safe and pleasant, these trips can be made quickly and efficiently by foot or bicycle (maybe the new tires are *for* the bicycle). In that case, our exercise regimen could easily be our walk or our bike ride, adding further efficiency to the day. If we don't have time to cook from scratch, the deli is so close that it's easy to stop in on the way home and pick up fresh foods prepared locally instead of relying on packaged products that were driven cross-country by truck or flown in from overseas. Perhaps some of the food we eat is even grown in our neighborhood. Our friends that come over for dinner are free to enjoy an extra beer or two because they can walk themselves home at the end of the evening. Obviously, the global economy is too efficient in too many ways for us to abandon it, but if we consume within a local footprint (including ordering goods over the Internet with delivery to our doorstep), the neighborhood framework can be very time- and carbon efficient as well as satisfying.

Clustering neighborhoods around transit further increases their positive impact. At the edge of Freiburg, Germany, for example, an innovative district called Vauban has been redeveloped around a vision of sustainability and car-free living. On most of its internal streets, walking and cycling are the preferred forms of travel. Along Vauban's main street small shops offer food and everyday goods and services, and many residents happily patronize these businesses on foot. A tram service connects the neighborhood to downtown Freiburg, a trip that is also only fifteen minutes by bike. Using a free-market approach, Vauban's developer did not place a limitation on car ownership but did unbundle the cost of parking spaces from the cost of housing.

According to the Vauban master plan, street parking, attached garages, and driveways are not permitted in the district. Residents who own cars are required to purchase a parking space in one of the structured garages at the community's edge for the equivalent of about twenty-eight thousand dollars. As a result, homes are more affordable, and 81 percent of Vauban residents choose not to own a car.[1] A transportation survey showed that 57 percent of car-free residents had actually gotten rid of their vehicles specifically in anticipation of the move to Vauban.[2] They travel instead by foot, tram, bicycle, or taxi, and many have access to car-share vehicles for the few occasions when they require a vehicle. According to one architect working in the district, Vauban has been the best-selling residential area in Freiburg, particularly because the quality of life it offers is perceived to be very high.[3]

A neighborhood that gives people access to what they need every day becomes a place that residents will use, identify with, and take pride in. Another excellent example of this can be found in New York City. Parts of Brooklyn are quite insular communities where many people live, work, and recreate entirely within their cultural community. Even in Manhattan, people seem to find identity at the neighborhood level, despite the wealth of interesting things in adjacent neighborhoods. A former New York City resident illustrated a common perspective among Manhattanites with following comment: "In the years I lived in SoHo in a 180-square-foot apartment on Sullivan Street,

I only ventured north of 45th once every couple of months. I vividly recall being invited to a party on a Friday night on the Upper West Side and thinking, 'No way, that is just too far!' It was about six stops away on the A train."

In Boston the Big Dig, which was fundamentally a (troubled) car-oriented project, paradoxically has revitalized surface neighborhoods and dramatically altered patterns of access and connectivity. Highway I-93 used to create an imposing pedestrian barrier between the North End Italian neighborhood and Government Center, which is a major tourism and employment destination. Even though the distance between the two was not great, the North End had limited transit service and was considered off the beaten path. When the highway was buried and a long narrow park constructed on top, the barrier disappeared. Within a few weeks people were flowing across the park by foot to access things on the other side. The neighborhood connectivity has been a boon to the North End's property values and businesses, and the improved access to the North End's charm has transformed Government Center from a rather sterile plaza into the gateway to the North End. Pedestrian trips have replaced car and transit trips as the best way to get between two parts of the city. In fact, it all seems like one neighborhood now, which would have been unimaginable prior to its completion in 2007.

The College Street area in Toronto provides another example of a complete neighborhood with a strong community identity, high desirability as a place to live, and a low-carbon footprint. It is primarily served by streetcar, although the subway runs parallel to College Street about five long blocks to the north. The area was originally built out with three-story narrow, single-family detached houses and duplexes. Flexibility in the zoning has allowed them to be converted to apartments and condos but still required that special care be taken to preserve neighborhood character at the street level.[4] Nearly all of the original structures have been preserved, but by accommodating renters (including students and young professionals), the zoning bylaw allowed for a new population capable of supporting the small business offerings within walking distance.[5] The new residential mix supports a wealth of shops and restaurants along College Street, including the continent's best selection of Portuguese custard tarts.

Not surprisingly, complete neighborhoods that are compact enough to support low-carbon access to goods and services usually involve higher-density living than is found in most of today's suburban environments. Unfortunately, many people believe that there are as many examples of "bad density" as there are of "good density." Planners and developers need to be constantly mindful of the imperative for compact neighborhoods to evolve in a way that is pleasing to people and that preserves the richness, detail, and practicality of the pedestrian experience. This is important not only so that people derive pleasure from walking and biking around their neighborhood but also to avoid giving density a bad name. Projects that add density without consideration for the human experience (or, conversely, that overregulate the human experience) are enduring drivers of antidensity sentiment. In chapter 10 we discuss this issue in a more general way when we address the critical importance of delighting consumers as we implement measures to achieve carbon efficiency.

HOW WE CAN MAKE GREAT NEIGHBORHOODS

STRATEGY #6: Adopt measures that make compact, mixed-use neighborhoods attractive places for people to live and work. Recognize that these neighborhoods are our most powerful tool for reducing vehicular CO_2 emissions.

Federal Government

Focus HUD funding on compact and complete neighborhoods that are well served by transit.

The department of Housing and Urban Development (HUD) has significant influence over the development of complete neighborhoods. The institution's mandate to increase homeownership, improve access to affordable housing, and support community development can be most effectively satisfied when HUD encourages projects designed to complement other existing uses within a particular neighborhood. The alternative—developing housing in greenfield areas—may result in lower initial land costs, but there is no guarantee that complementary retail services and amenities will follow. In many cases a single HUD project on its own may not attract the critical mass in people or income base to attract all the other components of a complete neighborhood. Directing HUD funds into neighborhoods that already have an adequate density of retail uses and other amenities may incur higher land costs, but these projects are more likely to be successful as complete neighborhoods.

This is not an abstract ideal. Rather, the strategy will deliver a positive bottom-line impact to the families HUD serves. As we mentioned in chapter 4 when discussing location-efficient mortgages, complete neighborhoods that are well served by transit can substantially reduce the need for car ownership.

The annual savings on car-related expenses, including monthly payments, insurance, maintenance, and fuel (in the range of eight thousand dollars per year per car, according to the AAA), can defray the additional cost of land in built-up areas within a matter of months or a few years.[6] Furthermore, many moderate and low-income family members have multiple jobs, which creates scheduling challenges with respect to running errands and taking care of children. Complete neighborhoods would serve the time needs of HUD's constituents better than dispersed patterns of living or compact patterns with little access to services, amenities, and jobs. Where families have an increased ability to pay for housing because the location helps them defray other expenses, HUD can reasonably justify its investment within a project pro forma of five to seven years.

This is not news to HUD, of course. In March 2009 the agency announced the formal partnership with the Department of Transportation (DOT) (mentioned in the Introduction) to promote sustainable communities through joint housing and transportation initiatives. The Environmental Protection Agency (EPA) joined the partnership several months later, emphasizing the connection between land use, transportation, and the environment, with respect to climate change. Key tenets of the partnership include goals to increase transportation choices, support existing communities rather than new development in rural areas, and invest in "healthy, safe and walkable neighborhoods."[7] This kind of alignment of policy and regulatory efforts at the federal level is an example of the kind of framework we need to ensure that housing and transportation initiatives complement one another to support land use and development for competitive, connected, and successful communities across the country.

State Governments

Review state environmental policy requirements to eliminate barriers to compact development and urban infill development.

Every state has its version of a set of policies meant to prevent new development from causing environmental degradation. Whether part of state environmental acts or simply embedded in the development permitting-evaluation processes, these policies establish minimum standards as well as review processes, such as environmental impact statements (EIS), to evaluate the effect of new projects. As a result, these policies have become the basis for a significant part of the regulation surrounding new development, and considerable case law has evolved dealing with state-level environmental issues.

This is positive in the sense that the regulatory environment is being harmonized across state and local jurisdictions, but it also presents risks in reacting quickly and in being overly prescriptive about the means of reaching the targets. Case law takes a long time to evolve in response to emerging greenhouse gas mitigation mandates. In the past few years, for instance, such books as *Growing Cooler* and *Moving Cooler* (both published by the nonprofit Urban Land Institute) have provided data that convincingly demonstrate that compact urban development is the number-one thing that can quickly impact carbon emissions in the United States at the lowest economic cost.[8] The great paradox is that the mountains of case law around our state environmental policies can work against this very thing. An example can be found in Washington State, where one of the unintended consequences of the State Environmental Policy Act (SEPA) is that lower-density projects tended to fare better under its criteria. As a result, many opponents of compact or high-density urban infill projects have used SEPA to try to block these new developments. In many ways SEPA has created additional barriers to compact development that do not exist for low-density or "sprawl" projects.

While leaving greenhouse gas target implementation to the creativity of local jurisdictions and the private sector is a good thing, overcoming the case law and fundamentally integrating carbon emission targets into the EIS analysis process likely requires more specific language in the state policy itself. The following provides specific suggestions for improving current state environmental protection legislation frameworks so that they support the development of complete neighborhoods.

Revise system boundaries so that environmental impact statements reflect the differing contributions of low- and high-density development.

Where state environmental policies prescribe an environmental goal, there needs to be a way to balance that goal with the overarching regional objective of promoting higher-density developments. For example, current environmental regulation often requires new developments to allocate a certain percentage of site surfaced areas to pervious surfaces to mitigate stormwater runoff. If, as is usually the case, there is no accounting for density-related factors in these regulations, high-density projects will fare poorly when tested against these rules; it just may not be feasible to allocate a large percentage of intensely developed property to pervious surfaces (even green spaces at ground level may be over basements or parking). Ironically, by absorbing more growth in the urban core, compact projects are the best vehicle for preserving undeveloped and highly pervious wild and working lands that are critical to watershed preservation.

One way to address this problem is to strike a balance between a system boundary that only includes the specified project (as Washington's SEPA currently does) and a broader perimeter that includes the city or the region. This balance would consider that while a suburban development of one hundred houses, each built on one acre of land, may have a high ratio of pervious surface and meet the SEPA threshold, its cumulative impervious surface area (in absolute terms and per person housed) is much higher than that of a close-in townhouse or cottage development. In suburban development the per-home footprints consist of the houses themselves, driveways, street surfaces connecting them, and their share of the impervious highway infrastructure linking their subdivision to other parts of the city; this total area dwarfs the per-townhouse coverage. In other words, the townhouse development has a higher ratio of impervious surfaces relative to its local area but a much lower amount of impervious surface relative to the region and relative to the number of inhabitants it houses.

Alter level of service (LOS) in environmental protection laws to include other modes and provide credit for increased intraneighborhood trips and nonmotorized trips.

A significant portion of the analysis in any EIS relates to level of service for automobiles. The logic goes something like this: if a project puts more people in a neighborhood, then by definition it puts more cars on the streets around the project. The developer is then responsible for costs of any road improvements (road widening, signalization, turn lanes, and so on) related to restoring the level of service back to where it was before the project. Chapter 3 discussed some of the flaws in this logic—most important, the fact that additional density is not purely additive to local car trips. It may—in a complete neighborhood—actually obviate the need for many of them. In addition, density supports additional and more cost-effective transit service and in turn enables trips to other parts of the region to be taken by transit rather than by single-occupancy vehicles (SOV).

State environmental protection legislation might do better to broaden its definition of "access." Currently, the LOS concept assumes that all access takes place by car. Car LOS is the proxy for how a given development will impact people's ability to get to the things they need. The implication is that increasing road capacity is the prerequisite to additional development, when in fact additional compact development within complete neighborhoods has been shown to actually reduce the need for road capacity. State environmental policies could be more effective if their definition of access included pedestrian, bicycle, and transit access.

What would this look like in practice? A broader definition of access would lead to LOS models that considered a "basket" of trips that people within the neighborhood might need to take (just as the consumer price index considers a "basket" of commonly consumed goods and services). Planners could analyze how many alternate modes of mobility can be used to complete that basket of trips, within a certain amount of time that people allocate to travel in one day. The basket approach would allow the possibility of additional car trips to be offset against the likelihood of replacement trips by walking, bicycling, or transit, if those possibilities are created simultaneously.

This approach may strike some readers as requiring quite a few behavioral assumptions. So, however, do the existing models for car trips. Data to predict car trips in a given area are typically gathered at the national level and then tweaked to local behavioral patterns; the analysis methods are fairly standardized and rigorous. Walk Score, a software product produced by the civic software company Front Seat, provides a model for measuring walkability access from many U.S. addresses on its Web site.[9] This and other tools like it could inform the analysis of nonvehicular access. An aggregate approach to access might even result in requiring developers to provide mitigation not in the form of road capacity improvements but instead in the form of additional bike lanes, wider sidewalks with better lighting, or transit-enabling infrastructure.

Provide credit under state environmental protection laws for decreased vehicle miles traveled (VMT) emissions as a positive environmental impact.

State environmental policies that regulate development might even go one step further, by considering the aggregate carbon impact of the change in mode split in the basket of trips serving the area before and after development. For instance, if 80 percent of trips in the basket were made in SOVs before the project and only 60 percent were made in SOVs after the project because of increased access options, the project might do better on carbon emissions from an aggregate EIS perspective. The improvement in the VMT carbon footprint of the neighborhood might offset some of the negative impacts with respect to infringement on view corridors or shadow studies (all of which are other parts of the SEPA analysis that frequently create challenges for higher-density projects).

If the basket of trips and its resulting carbon score were considered, we might eventually see state environmental protection laws helping to pave the way for compact infill projects to go forward more smoothly, rather than being used to block or challenge them as they frequently are today. An analysis showing improvement in VMT and carbon footprint resulting from a compact, complete neighborhood project would be a strong counterbalance to those who fear that infill projects have negative environmental consequences due to congestion. This would in turn raise the threshold for challenging high-density projects on state environmental policy grounds.

Invest in urban schools as a prerequisite to compact connected and complete neighborhoods.

On a completely different note, the decline of major urban centers in the United States has been driven in part by the disparity in quality between public schools in urban centers and those in suburbs and exurban areas. The problems with the country's education system are beyond the scope of this book, but there is no question that investment in the success of urban schools is a sine qua non of successful and complete urban neighborhoods. An analysis of almost any compact-density or high-density urban neighborhood shows many people gravitating there in their twenties, then leaving in their thirties, with some returning as empty nesters. A complete neighborhood strategy that meets lifelong human needs and fosters strong ties among residents cannot exist without strong urban schools. States that want to lower the carbon footprint of their built environment need to figure out how to get this right.

Local Governments

Create zoning that supports flexible mixed-use neighborhoods.

Local governments can also do a great deal to support complete neighborhoods. Since the 1940s, urban zoning and land use practices have tended to segregate land uses: one area is solely commercial, another is retail, another is multifamily housing, and another is single-family housing. The reality of human access patterns is that people need a little of all these things every day. Mixing uses within buildings, within city blocks, and especially within defined neighborhoods creates a sense of place and allows people to access multiple uses in a short space and time. Conversely, separating land into large, multiacre tracts dedicated to a single use creates homogenous areas that are usually only active during certain hours and makes it much more difficult for people to move between uses as their needs evolve over the course of the day.

One approach to this problem is to implement mixed-use zoning that requires retail at the ground level of all buildings in neighborhoods where density reaches a certain threshold. This has been moderately successful in Seattle's downtown. But in some cases that mandate has forced the development of unleasable retail space, because some sites—due to their shape, size, accessibility, safety concerns, or other factors—simply cannot support successful retail. A better model may be the one that will soon be adopted in some parts of Seattle's South Lake Union neighborhood. According to this new policy, most of the blocks can be developed as office, residential, or retail, either alone or in combination, but no specific use is prescribed. This allows for a more efficient market response to providing all the component amenities that people need in their day. In medium-density neighborhoods, where retail is not feasible at all street-front locations, the concept of retail hubs or "main streets"—which concentrate amenities serving a five- to ten-block radius—can work very well by creating both efficient access patterns for people to meet their needs and an active community center.

Employ creative strategies to "upzone" single-family neighborhoods to higher densities while preserving strong communities and a viable building stock.

Many close-in residential neighborhoods were originally zoned exclusively for single-family detached housing at a time when cities were smaller. As cities grow and close-in urban land becomes more valuable, single-family neighborhoods are faced with a challenge: upzone to allow more density, which leads to tearing down existing housing that may still be viable, or keep existing zoning in place, creating a low-density "doughnut" around the city center.

The doughnut approach limits the total number of people who can live close-in and drives up the cost of close-in housing beyond what many people can pay. It also tends to limit the viability of transit service, because expensive transit infrastructure needs to cut through relatively lower-density swaths of land. The fatter the low-density doughnut, the harder it is to build density on the outside of it, since it comes with little benefit in reduced commute times to and from the urban center.

How can creative zoning be used to increase the density of close-in, single-family neighborhoods? One alternative to upzoning that has had some success in several urban markets is the allowance for easy permitting of auxiliary dwelling units (sometimes known as "granny flats" or mother-in-law apartments) on existing single-family home sites. Within a fairly flexible envelope, they essentially allow a doubling of density within an existing single-family neighborhood. Auxiliary housing has the added benefit of preserving the materials and embodied energy of the principal dwelling unit, because it's one of the rare instances in which increasing density doesn't require replacing the existing structure (making it an excellent example of reuse at a neighborhood scale).

This strategy also tends to increase neighborhood permanence and social cohesion by providing flexibility that allows extended families to stay connected or encourages a mix of ages and incomes within a small geographic area. All of these things in turn have been correlated with increased investment in the neighborhood, decreased violence and petty crime, increases in social capital, and decreases in the incidence of depression among residents.[10] Auxiliary units can also be a source of added income or savings for a homeowner who chooses to rent out the unit or uses it to accommodate extended family. Backyard cottages are certainly not a panacea, but they do represent an example of a creative and workable solution to increasing urban density in a way that promotes complete neighborhoods. Other examples of creative zoning solutions within existing neighborhoods include the addition of multifamily or office development over retail on the shopping street of existing residential neighborhoods, the introduction of office and residential uses into close-in industrial areas, allowances to convert single-family homes into duplexes or triplexes, and elimination of minimum lot sizes and subdivision restrictions.

In many cities on-site parking requirements create the need for consumers to make a choice between yards and green space in suburban neighborhoods versus small, urban residential sites with little or no yard. Reducing or even eliminating minimum parking requirements in close-in neighborhoods, however, allows for shared green spaces, even in compact development patterns. A few years ago, the Seattle City Council issued a call for ideas to improve the model for townhouses as part of an effort to update the city's approach to multifamily zoning.[11] This process led to criticism of the current code: its requirements for green space and a minimum of two dedicated off-street parking spaces per unit, however well-meaning, are both stumbling blocks that inhibit compact density. The parking requirement often forces unwelcome design compromises, such as unusable "spare bedrooms" behind the garage. Furthermore, the current green space requirement often results in small, useless "corrals" of grass at the street level, separated from the sidewalk by a six-foot fence.

According to Seattle architect Robert Humble, who has worked for years on innovative compact residential projects (and who participated in the city's townhouse improvement initiative), changing the green space requirement to allow these spaces to be located entirely on the roof (as a roof deck) "would allow additional lot coverage and make the green space more usable due to the access to light and views." Humble says that eliminating the parking requirement "is a very tough sell politically, but one that needs to be pushed."[12] We couldn't agree more. Parking minimums effectively force parking to be bundled with shelter, driving up the cost and reducing customer choice.

There is a way to address both problems at once, however. If the parking requirement were eliminated, designs could allow for a usable yard that would be shared between two to eight dwellings. Reducing or eliminating parking minimums allows people developing compact, close-in sites to make the choice of offering a shared yard rather than a second parking space. Some critics charge that fewer onsite parking stalls results in increased on-street parking, but parallel parking by the curb actually has the benefit of causing traffic to move more slowly, resulting in a safer pedestrian experience. It bears mentioning that street parking has a huge invisible cost of its own and is another prime example of subsidies for cars. Cities pay to pave and maintain countless acres of street parking at high real economic cost to residents. Street parking is also a large contributor to watershed degradation in that it can represent up to a third of impervious surface in many parts of cities.

Provide lower carbon zoning solutions even for new single-family developments by encouraging mix of uses, limited lot sizes, and transit connectivity.

Despite every wishful strategy promoting urban density, many people will still want to live in a single-family detached house and will drive as far as they must to get one. Even if cities and neighborhoods shift to more complete, compact, and desirable patterns of development over the next ten to fifteen years, residential growth of single-family communities is also likely to continue to increase. It's necessary, then, to think about how cities can support good alternatives in single-family housing as a parallel strategy to encouraging compact density. Enabling master-planned communities that create compact, mixed-use suburban neighborhoods therefore needs to be part of the overall development goal for cities and regions. Sustainable single-family neighborhoods need to have eight or more houses per acre; pedestrian or bicycle access to basic amenities, such as pharmacies, grocery stores, restaurants, and coffee shops; and connections to transit either directly (as in Germany's Vauban district) or through a network of park-and-rides, vanpools, or connector shuttles.

Subiaco, an upscale suburban community located a few kilometers west of Perth in Western Australia, provides one contemporary example of how these considerations can transform development even outside of the city. Perth is a sprawling and car-centric metropolis not unlike many found in the United States. But since 1990, the city has made development of a strong regional rail system a priority of local government, and Subiaco is one destination where the rail connection has made way for very successful transit-oriented redevelopment.[13] In the area surrounding the underground Subi-Centro rail station, a former industrial area has been redeveloped into a flourishing, compact, walkable, and in-demand neighborhood offering retail, jobs, family-oriented green space, and residences. It's important to note that one key factor in the Subi-Centro redevelopment was a 1994 act of Parliament creating the Subiaco Redevelopment Agency and exempting the area from local planning conditions and requirements so that this intense development could take place. Although not all residents of Subiaco live adjacent to the rail station and about 40 percent live in single-family detached homes, the rail connection between Perth and Subiaco (and many other communities in Western Australia) has greatly reduced dependence on automobiles for all residents.[14]

Suburban "eco village" developments are another strategy being tested in some markets in the United States and elsewhere. Sonoma Mountain Village, a mixed-use community currently under development forty miles north of San Francisco, is one example. With a vision of creating an environment where residents can live sustainably by default, the developer is planning a community in which all residents live within a five-minute walk of grocery stores, childcare services, and other daily amenities. Many jobs will exist right on-site, and a nearby light-rail stop offers residents an easy connection to the city. This developer hopes that the project will not only serve the residents within it but will also attract business from the surrounding communities, where development is more sprawling. While it doesn't solve all problems of low-density land use patterns, providing high-intensity mixed-use cores in suburban areas is no doubt a step in the right direction, as it allows residents in these areas a choice of modes in meeting many of their daily needs.

Environmental Nonprofits

Help neighborhoods and individuals understand the benefits of increased density.

Many people resist infill development, regardless of its potential to increase access within neighborhoods. Capitalizing on the new opportunities for access that come with infill development typically requires people to change their patterns of behavior, which is challenging. In the past many environmental nonprofits have focused on preserving rural lands and carbon sinks, largely ignoring the other side of the coin, which is to make sure that cities can accommodate more density. More recently, some groups have taken up the task of working with neighborhoods to make them more receptive of infill development. In Seattle, Citytank.org, Great City, and Forterra (the organization formerly known as the Cascade Land Conservancy) are three such organizations that have realized that compact neighborhoods go hand-in-hand with reducing carbon emissions. They work with community organizations and neighborhood leaders to draw the connection between compact growth and sustainability, and help the public understand how additional density and services can improve their access, walkability, and general quality of life over the long term.

NEIGHBORHOODS IN A NUTSHELL

Mixed-use neighborhoods tend to be self-contained and can thus foster the strong sense of identity and community that make them great places to live. They are also carbon efficient because they reduce VMT, and the denser they are, the more pronounced this effect. All levels of government should encourage the evolution of these types of neighborhoods both proactively and by removing existing policy and regulatory barriers. Environmental nonprofits need to help the public understand that compact and appealing urban areas are critical to preserving green spaces and promoting carbon efficiency.

CHAPTER 7

SPACES FOR NATURE

Everybody needs beauty as well as bread, places to play in and pray in, where nature may heal and give strength to body and soul.

—JOHN MUIR

Bill Reed, a prominent systems ecologist who works with developers on built environment projects, gets his clients to adopt strategies that radically change their original plans for development. More specifically, he decides what attributes a project should have in order to fit in with its natural environment, and he persuades developers to transform their thinking in this direction and convinces them that they can still be profitable. How does he do this? To really see the possibilities of working in sync with the natural environment, and to feel good about it at a "gut-instinct" level, Reed explains, people need to "date nature." "We've mistreated nature for so long, pushed her back and neglected her. Just like if you do that to a girlfriend, pretty soon you wind up not wanting to see her at all, you don't want to include her in your plans, or go to parties where you might see her. You wind up kind of embarrassed and so you create a social environment that she's not part of at all. In order to get people to even want to engage with nature, we need to get over the fact that we've all neglected her, and start dating her again. Go out into nature and find joy in it, and remember what's worth preserving."[1]

Inspiration

Regardless of how you feel about "dating nature," it's hard to disagree with Bill's point: If people don't have opportunities to connect with and get to know nature, it's less likely they will be motivated to find new ways of doing things that have lower emissions impacts and are better for the environment overall. In other words, not only do we need economic frameworks that support carbon-efficiency and broad buy-in to achieving it, we also need as many people as possible to be inspired by and passionate about the goal. We need more than just creativity from scientists; we also need ideas from every quarter about how to transform economic processes and human behaviors. By integrating nature into the built environment, we can ensure that every person has the opportunity to connect with natural resources and processes.

To deal with climate change in the limited time frame we have, we may even need ideas that go beyond carbon-neutral, that are capable of actually reducing net carbon emissions. We know they exist because they are all around us in the natural world; photosynthesis is a good example found in every backyard. Biomimetics, also called biomimicry, is a field of engineering and design devoted to using inspiration from natural systems to inform the creation of products that meet human needs. As the world's fastest train, Japan's Shinkansen Bullet Train is a mechanical marvel, but it also provides a good example of how engineers can learn about efficiency from nature. When it was originally brought into service, the train's speed caused huge sonic booms as the train collided with air in underground tunnels. Designers re-created the front end of the train using the beak of a kingfisher as a model, since the bird is able to travel quickly through wind and water with minimal friction and noise. The new design is not only quieter; it uses 15 percent less energy and travels 10 percent faster.[2] Because biomimetic designers look to replicate processes found in the natural world where all waste becomes a nutrient in a new cycle, biomimetic systems often minimize side effects and are less environmentally disruptive.[3]

Fixation

Setting aside spaces for nature also provides direct and immediate environmental benefit. Natural landscapes, particularly those that have rich vegetative growth, are carbon fixers. When plants photosynthesize, they use the sun's energy to metabolize CO_2 molecules from the atmosphere and turn them into long molecules that have many atoms of carbon linked together and that become the mass of the plant. The freed-up oxygen is released into the atmosphere. (Conversely, when we burn a piece of wood, or any other hydrocarbon such as oil or coal, the process consumes oxygen to break apart the long carbon chains, and CO_2 is released into the atmosphere.) Healthy natural landscapes that grow quickly reduce atmospheric CO_2 and counteract global warming. The Amazon rainforest, for example, is one of the richest natural environments in terms of plant volume and growth per hectare. Its loss significantly reduces the ability of the planet to reabsorb the carbon that we put into the atmosphere. Boreal forests and ocean algae colonies are other essential carbon sinks and are also threatened by deforestation and pollution. Losing these resources further accelerates our move toward a climate tipping point.

Urban trees and green spaces, while smaller in scale than boreal or Amazon forests, also contribute to carbon fixation. Because an urban tree typically grows to a larger size than its "wild" counterpart, it contains about four times more carbon than an average tree in the wild.[4] In addition to the carbon they sequester, urban trees can make a three to four times larger contribution to carbon reduction when planted in locations where they help conserve energy by, for example, creating shade for buildings.[5] A study conducted on homes in southern California in 2004 estimated that three shade trees (two on the west side and one on the east) could reduce a homeowner's annual cooling costs by between 10 and 50 percent.[6]

Beautiful, Livable Cities

There are other, less tangible but perhaps even more important benefits from incorporating nature into cities. People love—and gravitate to—natural spaces. Whether they are wild or highly manicured, urban spaces for nature significantly increase land values in surrounding areas and help mitigate the cost of setting the space aside. Chicago's Millennium Park is an excellent example of a transformative urban space for nature. In the early days of the city, the area along the Lake Michigan waterfront that the park now occupies was a rail yard. As the city developed, some of the rail yard capacity was moved further away from the city center, but several major rail lines and related parking lots remained, effectively creating a barrier between the city and the lake.

In the early 1990s Mayor Richard M. Daley devised a plan to make a new waterfront park part of his legacy. Over the following years, the city regained control of the land from the Illinois Central Railroad (which donated its rights, title, and interest to the city), designed the park to accommodate two underground subway lines and replace the surface parking capacity with underground structured parking, and raised public and private funds to finance the project. The 24.5-acre park, built at a total cost of $490 million, opened in 2005 and is a showcase of architecture, monumental sculpture, and landscape design. It is now the hub and the pride of the city and has increased surrounding property values nearly threefold, creating an estimated $1.4 billion of value.[7]

This value proposition applies on a smaller scale to countless other urban natural spaces across the country—from playgrounds to large parks with wilderness hiking trails, to pocket parks on odd empty lots, to tree-lined streets and community gardens in dense city neighborhoods. Spaces for nature make urban living comfortable and desirable. As we discussed in chapters 4 and 6, public spaces like urban parks play a heightened role in compact communities where private spaces are smaller. If we don't offer people good alternatives, many will keep driving until they can afford that backyard. Successful green spaces are not necessarily large, but they should be plentiful. Safe and clean parks can also indirectly strengthen neighborhood connectivity, leading to safer streets, more community stability, and ultimately more community reinvestment in a vibrant and satisfying neighborhood.

RECOGNIZING GOOD SPACES FOR NATURE

What do people need to find in cities to overcome the perception that they need a large, private yard in the suburbs? Parks are important, but there are many different kinds of parks, and there are also many other ways to find nature in outdoor spaces. To understand the array of possibilities for making nature present in urban areas, it helps to stratify the needs and wants of people by age group: young children, adolescents, and adults.

Young children need safe, clean, and not-too-crowded playgrounds that aren't far from where they live. Interestingly, the aesthetics of these parks are important mostly to parents, and because the parents determine whether and how often their young children will use the parks—whether those parks are a viable substitute for a private backyard outside of the city—the aesthetic aspect cannot be neglected. However, as we've noticed in our own child-rearing experiences, and as authors Christopher Alexander, Sara Ishikawa, and Murray Silverstein so rightly pointed out in *A Pattern Language*, "Any kind of playground which disturbs, or reduces, the role of imagination and makes the child more passive . . . may look nice, may be clean, may be safe, may be healthy—but it just cannot satisfy the fundamental need which play is all about. . . . Huge abstract sculptured play-lands . . . are not just sterile; they are useless."[8] The authors go on to suggest (and we can recall from our own childhoods) that the best playgrounds have lots of raw materials to feed the imagination: wood, tools, grass, trees, nets, ropes, rocks, boxes, and water.

Adolescents use urban outdoor spaces mostly as sports fields, on both an organized and an ad-hoc basis. In many cases this age group doesn't make much use of a backyard even if they have one; they are too preoccupied with hanging out with their friends, and most of them don't want to do that in their own backyard. Adolescents need safe, open fields and, recognizing that families may spend considerable time at these fields attending sporting events, the more these areas provide a nature experience, the better.

For adults, enclosed parks with trees, water, grass, wild areas, and spots for picnics are obviously a good thing, but there are a lot of other options that can also appeal to them. Many adults like to experience nature by walking or cycling in it. There are countless examples of extremely popular urban paths along shorelines, waterways, ravines, or even old railway rights-of-way.[9] The interesting thing about some of the most successful of these is that they often consume little more land than a few times the width of their trail, and they are cheek-to-jowl with the city (this latter attribute may be a key aspect of their popularity). Even more simply, adults can experience and enjoy nature while walking a tree-lined street, passing an attractive mini-park or yard, or viewing a cityscape that includes natural plants and flowers on rooftops and terraces, in attractive containers, or even climbing the sides of walls.

In 2008, at the height of the recession, 59 percent of Seattle voters approved a ballot measure to generate an additional $146 million in property taxes over six years for parks and green spaces.[10] The parks levy dedicated additional funds to the creation of urban green spaces in neighborhoods that were underserved by parks, many of which were also becoming more dense with the infill of townhouses, mid-rise condo and apartment projects, and cottage housing. Many of the parks that will be created with these funds are quite small—only one or two former house lots—but they aim to provide most residents with access to a neighborhood park within a four- to five-block walk of their homes. The small size and neighborhood orientation of these green areas have made the projects particularly appealing, as a result galvanizing community investment in their creation, maintenance, and programming.

People who live in cities also need spaces for nature outside of the cities.

Urban green spaces cannot replicate the grandeur and inspiration of forests, prairies, lakes, rivers, mountains, or an unbroken stretch of starlit night sky. The U.S. system of national and state parks provides important opportunities for people to come out of the city and "date nature."

Forterra (the organization formerly known as the Cascade Land Conservancy) is a nonprofit organization that was founded in 1989 to preserve natural spaces around the Puget Sound area and into the Cascade Mountains. Forterra originally focused on rural spaces exclusively, raising money to purchase rural land and keep it permanently wild. However, recognizing that population patterns change and that the Puget Sound area continues to attract people from across the country, Forterra also became concerned about urban development and redevelopment. Many in the organization have come to see urban density as an enabler of rural preservation and as an important element of climate stability. The organization has spoken out in support of new proposals for compact development that also promote great urban public spaces. It has also worked with the cities and the state to develop a complementary system of transfer development rights (known as TDRs) that makes preserving rural green space a viable strategy in the market.

HOW WE CAN HAVE SPACES FOR NATURE

STRATEGY #7: Recognize the value inherent in public green space both as a carbon sink and as a critical means for making the built environment inviting to individuals and usable by families. Structure developments and neighborhoods with accessible outdoor recreational space, and foster access to wilderness parks.

Federal and State Governments

Continue to invest in national and state parks that are accessible to people who live in urban centers.

Since Yellowstone National Park was established in 1872 as the world's first national park, the United States has built a network of fifty-eight national parks comprising millions of acres of wilderness, all of which are stunning showcases for nature.[11] States have done their part as well, adding more than sixty-six hundred state parks that had more than 725 million visits in 2009 (an average of 2.5 visits per citizen).[12] But since 2001, only two new (and relatively small) national parks have been established; the previous twenty years saw eight new national parks, while a total of nineteen were established in the two decades between 1961 and 1980.[13]

State parks are seeing their attendance grow while their operating budgets shrink.[14] During the fifty-year period since 1960, the urbanized population of the United States has grown from 125 million to in excess of 225 million.[15] Clearly, while the demand for natural recreational spaces has been increasing, we have reduced our commitment to making parks available. In many places it's very difficult for a family to find a state park campsite on a weekend in the summer; in Washington State, for example, a substantial portion of sites are filled nine months in advance, as soon as the reservation system opens for that day. It's hard to expect people to give up their acreage in Enumclaw, or even their big backyard in the suburbs, when it's so difficult to get access to a park on a summer weekend. Investing in state and national parks within reasonable distances of major metropolitan areas pays dividends in supporting individuals' choices for increasing urbanization while still maintaining access to the great outdoors.

Quantify the value of national and state forests as carbon sinks and manage them accordingly.

National and state forests are also an important component of the public open-space resource, both as carbon sinks and for their value as artifacts of nature. However, some state and national forests have been severely depleted by logging and will take decades to regenerate. To make matters worse, clear-cutting is the predominant logging method. Besides being destructive to ecosystems, clear-cutting increases landslide and avalanche risk and makes spaces unusable by (and unattractive to) the public. If national and state governments are in fact the stewards of the public good, they should ascribe an economic value to trees and vegetation as part of an overall national emissions management strategy. Each hectare of forest would thus have a "carbon sink value" (correlated with the carbon tax) that the government would need to recoup as part of selling the timber. If the forest didn't have enough commercial value to cover the loss of its value as a carbon sink, the economics of the situation would cause it to remain intact.

Some economists are already hard at work on projects that are exploring how this quantification could be done. In 2008 researchers at a Tacoma, Washington–based environmental think tank called Earth Economics produced a study called "A New View of the Puget Sound Economy." The report examined the economic value that the region's natural resources (including Puget Sound, natural wetlands, and others) contribute in the form of benefits like clean drinking water, flood control, carbon sequestration, erosion protection, fish, recreation, and even improved public health. The authors of the study concluded that the ecosystems surrounding the region's cities were worth at least $305 billion, or as much as $2.6 trillion, and were careful to state that their analysis left out many benefits that were more difficult to quantify. In placing a value on ecosystems, the economic team hoped to provide governments and other institutions with information that could help shape policy for preserving natural resources or quantifying and charging for the impact of pollution.[16]

Local Governments

Keep local parks safe and plentiful.

If we really want people to feel good about compact-density living, cities must eliminate common barriers to using public space. If urban parks are truly to serve as a replacement for yards, they need to be close-by to everyone. Even if a park is in good condition, it fails to create value for households located more than typical walking distance away (five to ten blocks). Large distances between public spaces effectively prevent people living in apartments or condominiums from accessing them with ease and continuity.

Local parks don't create value either if they aren't safe and clean. Local jurisdictions need to allocate adequate budgets to maintain and patrol parks to prevent vandalism, drug dealing, and drug use. If parks become unsafe, they fail to provide families with a viable alternative to a private backyard. Funding should also be allocated to outfit parks with some of the amenities of a backyard. Comfortable seating, grilling areas, play areas, and sheltered spaces all enhance a park's appeal and encourage its use.

Incorporate nature into cities in as many ways as possible.

Beyond parks, cities and their citizens need to think broadly about fostering the many other ways of providing access to nature. Walking trails are probably more important to most adults than parks. Trees reduce carbon, provide shelter for birds, and bring a strong sense of the beauty of nature to people even when viewed from a distance. Well-tended gardens, planted boulevards, potted plants, and flower baskets embedded throughout downtowns and other high-traffic destinations are much more than tourist attractions. They play an important role in making residents feel good about their city, and that's a critical factor in keeping them living in it.

Revise zoning so that interblock transfer of development rights programs and reduced parking requirements create opportunities for shared urban green spaces and parks.

Finally, to encourage open public spaces, cities should reexamine their internal zoning codes and TDR policies to make sure that the limits on TDR don't discourage or block opportunities for placing parks adjacent to high-density areas. As discussed in chapter 6, minimum parking space requirements can also result in an entire compact project being surrounded by surface parking or vehicle access lanes, leaving no room for shared spaces for nature.

Transfers of development rights can also be used to allow private rural landowners to benefit from conserving forests and farmland within the region. TDR credits give landowners in rural areas the opportunity to realize the development value of their land while preserving it as open space or working land, by allowing them to sell all or some of their development rights to a landowner in an area targeted for growth. Through this transaction the purchaser gains a "bonus" in development rights that adds value to his or her property. The rural landowner receives financial compensation, and a permanent conservation easement is placed on the rural land.[17] (In most cases, the owner is still allowed to farm the land, harvest timber, and so on as long as the land remains undeveloped.)

TDR policies can complement sound zoning and allow rural landowners to preserve their land as a working natural resource without forcing them to involuntarily relinquish their property rights, as a straight down-zoning of the property would. The market value of development rights is determined by the seller and negotiated with the buyer just as in most conventional real estate transactions. TDRs have been successful in ways that zoning and regulation simply cannot match: for example, the conservation easements achieved through TDRs are permanent, while changes in zoning can shift according to the political climate. TDRs can also be a tool for encouraging historical preservation, open space, or other community interests related to redevelopment within an urban area.

Environmental Nonprofits

Advocate for green spaces in urban environments.

Environmental nonprofits can be particularly effective advocates for including nature and green spaces in urban environments. They should focus not just on the quantity of space but also on the quality of space. Through outreach and education these groups can help the public understand how the development of cities doesn't compete with or threaten the conservation agenda; rather, it is part of a holistic solution.

Developers

Leverage innovative zoning to provide semiprivate or shared open spaces in projects.

Intensive small-scale development projects will typically rely on city parks to provide shared open spaces. However, in compact development projects or even in larger civic projects, there are opportunities to provide spaces for nature that can add value to the finished product. City code requirements have tended to be prescriptive about the size of open spaces that developers need to include, but not about the quality. Cities need to remove barriers to creating spaces for nature in the ground plane of a project so that developers have a broader range of options, but there is also room for developers to think in innovative ways about customer value.

Find ways to make compact development work for families.

How do people use their yards? Can six or ten families share one yard and still use it in essentially the same way? What would that look like? These are important questions, because research into demographic patterns shows that although many young people choose to live close-in to urban cores, they often move to the suburbs once they have children. Some return when they are empty-nesters, but at that point there is a real inertia challenge to overcome. Families with small children need to be able to let their children go outside and know they are contained and safe. Ideally, parents must be able to see or hear their children from indoors so that they can keep track of what's going on. Parents also need to be able to get out to their children in a flash if anything goes wrong. With all of these characteristics in place, a yard shared by five to ten families would not only be feasible; it might even be preferable because it would give children a place to play with their friends in a place that was highly visible but still sheltered from the street.

Many cities in Europe, such as Barcelona and Paris, encourage a style of development referred to as "perimeter block" with an inner courtyard completely enclosed by the buildings around it. Not only does this create a very safe place for children, it is also one of the most compact ways to provide housing. Unfortunately, largely due to parking requirements, few urban projects in the United States have this form. As a result, most families buy two cars and move out of downtown, significantly ratcheting up their cost structure as well as their carbon footprint for the next twenty years. There's a great opportunity here for residential developers to listen to the voice of customers (who, as it happens, more often than not are committed to the environment and don't especially *like* dealing with traffic congestion) and offer them solutions that create high value on a small footprint.

SPACES FOR NATURE IN A NUTSHELL

Ubiquitous access to green spaces is a prerequisite to making urban environments attractive places for people to live. Nature is not incompatible with compact cities; it is a prerequisite to successful urban development. Urban parks are important, especially for younger children, but a strong sense of the beauty and comfort of nature can also be achieved by incorporating greenery into cityscapes through things like trees, pea patches, nature walkways on narrow strips of land, and hanging flower baskets. When beautiful cities are supplemented with reasonable access to wilderness parks, people can be very comfortable in compact urban environments.

CHAPTER 8

ON-SITE LIFE CYCLES

The first rule of sustainability is to align with natural forces, or at least not try to defy them.

—PAUL HAWKEN

n some ways buildings and neighborhoods operate like living organisms. They require inputs like water and energy, which travel through their massive circulatory systems of plumbing and wiring, and at the end of that process, they output wastes. Most of us are used to thinking of these input and output systems in a linear way: we pay monthly bills for the water and energy that come into our homes, and we send outputs down the drain. "On-site life cycles" refers to the idea that energy and potable water can be generated, used or transformed, and treated within a fairly small system boundary before being released back to the surroundings in a harmless way. Although some of the technologies for achieving this outcome are still in the developmental stages, many others have been proven and are well established, particularly in cities outside the United States, where the need for compact, decentralized, resource-efficient infrastructure has spurred innovation and implementation.

On-site life cycles are fundamentally concerned with access and infrastructure, and in that way this principle is parallel to the notion of complete neighborhoods described in chapter 6. But whereas complete neighborhoods are about access to consumer goods and services and social networks, the principle of on-site life cycles is about access to water, energy, and sanitation. Just as access to goods and services could be achieved either with a great deal of infrastructure and driving about, or with relatively little carbon impact, so can access to water, energy, and sanitation occur with either a great deal of delivery infrastructure or a relatively smaller, localized amount. A key difference between the two principles, however, is that in our modern economy the supply chain of many goods has become global because of production advantages in certain parts of the world. On the other hand, most inhabitable places have local access to fresh water (rain, wells, surface water) and energy (solar, wind, combustion). In many places the concept of on-site life cycles for energy and water may be much more achievable than the notion of neighborhood-scale supply chains for goods.

Off-site life cycles—which is to say, centralization of fresh water and energy generation and centralized treatment of sewage—are relatively new inventions in human history. Up until a few hundred years ago, most people settled in places near fresh water and in places where solar energy or combustion energy (usually in the form of forests) was adequate to support food growth and provide heat. In other words, water and energy were delivered with no infrastructure at all. As urban areas grew, local water sources became polluted, adjacent forests were depleted, and untreated surface sewage became a public health problem. This led to centralized sewage and garbage collection, remotely sourced and distributed water, and finally the development of electrical and other energy distribution infrastructures. These developments have made much greater densities of human habitation possible.

But this infrastructure comes at a high economic price. The "magic" of water flowing from faucets and emptying down the drain and of energy available from an outlet or a gas main has made us much less aware of our consumption of both the resources themselves and the infrastructure capacity required to bring them to us. Citywide water systems carry an enormous energy cost. Municipalities around the United States spend between 25 and 50 percent of their total electricity budgets on conveying and treating water and wastewater.[1] Likewise, combustion power plants often use large amounts of water to cool the plant machinery. So the two resource problems go hand in hand. According to the National Resource Defense Council, reducing water use is one of the cheapest strategies for conserving energy, and in a virtuous circle conserving energy would further reduce demand for municipal water.[2]

Unfortunately, inefficiencies are rampant in our modern water systems, and one of the main reasons for this is that their costs are not transparent to the end user. Much of the current infrastructure in the United States was built with various influxes of federal subsidies and grants and is more than fifty years old. Many water systems need replacement, and some leak away more than 25 percent of the water they treat. In 2003 the EPA estimated that investments of $270 billion over the next twenty years would be required to rebuild these systems and meet future needs. The situation for sewage systems is no better. The 2003 EPA estimate stated that $200 billion would need to be invested between 2003 and 2023 to update systems and control wastewater pollution.[3]

Current water and sewage tariffs are often not structured to fully amortize initial investments, and prices are similarly inadequate to build the necessary reserves needed to replace aging infrastructure.[4] To make matters worse, in some jurisdictions no usage charge is assessed at all, and 19 percent of water tariffs currently in effect actually give users a discount when they use more water (although this percentage has declined from 45 percent of tariff structures in 1992).[5] In Canada, where per capita water consumption is second only to the United States and the infrastructure is in similar disrepair, 43 percent of Canada's domestic water users pay a flat rate and an additional 12 percent are rewarded with lower rates when usage is higher. In a 2008 report on water consumption, the Conference Board of Canada stated: "Excessive water consumption in Canada can be attributed to the lack of widespread water conservation practices, as well as pricing that does not promote efficiency. In many cases, Canadians pay less for water than the actual cost of processing and delivery."[6]

If the price for water and sewage is not reflective of the true cost of providing these services, the market cannot make economically efficient choices about consumption. However, water usage has been shown in numerous studies, both in the United States and elsewhere, to vary consequentially with price, so we could reasonably expect a "true" price for water to reduce water usage.[7] Maybe with such a change the United States might even lose its leading position as the world's largest per capita user of water.

We often tend to lose sight of the fact that centralized distribution networks have unavoidable built-in inefficiencies. Many states generate a substantial portion of their electricity from the combustion of fossil fuels, a process that results in some of the energy being wasted as heat. Transmitting the electricity over power lines also creates losses. When that electricity is used to power a clothes dryer or a water heater, it is reconverted to heat, resulting in further losses. Water conveyance can be inefficient as well. Even new underground sewer pipes inevitably allow some leakage, which means that untreated effluent can leach into the groundwater and that some groundwater enters the pipes along their path. Energy at the treatment plant is then wasted treating clean groundwater mixed in with the wastewater.[8]

On-site life cycles impact carbon emissions in a positive way because they reduce the embodied emissions of large infrastructure projects, they avoid energy losses in transmission, they can minimize the energy required to treat sewage, and they have the potential to use renewable forms of energy or to generate energy from waste streams.

In their simplest form, on-site life cycles can exist at a building level. A composting toilet is one good, if not mainstream, example of an on-site waste-management cycle. Life cycles can also be implemented at a campus or neighborhood level, as in the case of a local waste bioreactor that produces combustible gas or a building heated with excess heat from an adjacent data center.

Although there are significant differences between building-level and neighborhood-level strategies, both change the role of the building or neighborhood they serve within the traditional distribution network. They represent a new way of thinking about utility service delivery: in these systems the end point in the network can be a net producer of value, rather than a consumer of value. This is a huge paradigm shift for utilities, and as a result, the traditional rules of engagement have created substantial barriers to on-site life cycles. This chapter discusses the nature of some of these barriers and how to mitigate them or eliminate them altogether so that the market can explore alternatives for reducing capacity utilization or even allowing certain users to create rather than to consume value at the outermost points of the distribution network.

RECOGNIZING OPPORTUNITIES FOR ON-SITE LIFE CYCLES

Despite the institutional barriers, there are numerous historical and current examples of on-site life cycles. Gardeners and farmers who compost organic by-products and thereby turn them into an input that increases the productivity of their land are exercising one traditional on-site solution. Another decades-old approach that has earned a lot of press in recent years is the use of waste vegetable oil to power converted diesel vehicles. Creative drivers source their oil from local food establishments, converting what would have been a waste product into a fuel that's both cheaper and cleaner burning than fossil fuel. These two simple examples illustrate two of the interesting things about on-site life cycles: they often use waste streams as an input to value-producing processes, and they can provide small-scale test beds for innovation.

On a much larger scale, the city of Stockholm incinerates more than 75 percent of its garbage at a facility located just five miles from its downtown. The city uses the electricity generated from incineration and also captures and reuses the heat that is thrown off in the process to provide district heating to about one hundred thousand households and business customers.[9] This local solution means the city requires far less landfill space (after accounting for recycling and biological waste treatment, only about 3 percent of municipal waste is sent to a landfill) and uses less energy to transport its garbage. On-site or local waste management also has an emergent or unintended behavioral benefit: it helps make people more aware of the quantities and types of products they put in the garbage. Untold numbers of batteries and other hazardous products are sent to landfills every year in the United States; it's quite likely, however, that people would think twice about putting them in the garbage if they were to be burned within five miles of their homes.

Another good example of private sector on-site energy generation can be found at the New Belgium Brewing Company, headquartered in Fort Collins, Colorado. New Belgium uses the methane produced by its on-site wastewater treatment process to fuel a combined heat and power generator that provides heat and electricity back to the brewery.[10] When running at full power, the generator can contribute 15 percent of the brewery's electricity needs.

Most inhabited parts of the world have some potential for on-site water access through such sources as rivers, lakes, underground aquifers, or rainwater. The traditional method for disposal of wastewater (filtered through soil or reused for watering plants) is not viable in densely populated areas. However, technologies now exist to engineer small-scale treatment of wastewater at a building or campus level. Among the more common options are bioreactors, living machines, and constructed wetlands.[11] These mechanisms essentially accelerate natural processes in a compact, odor-free environment to break down waste into usable byproducts.

To derive the benefits of an on-site cycle, a building or neighborhood doesn't have to go completely off the grid with respect to water use. Even a small reduction in consumption or wastewater production creates a benefit. One of the easiest ways to reuse water is to segregate inputs by quality. In the water industry, people refer to potable water (water that is clean enough to drink), grey water (water that is clean enough to water plants, flush the toilet, or wash clothing), and black water (water that is used to transport toxic products or human waste). While cooking and drinking water require a high level of purity (and regulation) for health and safety, grey water or rainwater is sufficient for many other uses for water. One of the largest burdens on the clean water distribution and sewage collection network is that a huge amount of clean water is transported along with the dirty water, without its having been used to its potential. When we turn on the shower and wait for the water to heat up, for instance, we are flushing perfectly clean water down the drain and getting no use at all out of it. This water could easily be reused for other household needs.

High-tech solutions for this exist: temperature-sensitive valves can prevent water from flowing out of the tap until a threshold temperature is reached, eliminating the loss of heated and clean water down the shower drain.[12] But there are good low-tech solutions as well: in multistory houses where the shower is upstairs, shower wastewater (a large source of grey water in most households) can be reused at the ground floor with the installation of a low-tech tank and gravity-fed system. Installing a system like this as a one-time retrofit requires code exceptions and can get expensive (because adoption is low and as a result of code restrictions). It is less costly to include a system in a newly constructed house, but generally those who install grey water systems do so out of concern for the environment and not necessarily because of the cost savings. If this technology were widely adopted, however, the payback would be substantially better, just as low-flush toilets became cost-competitive once they were widely installed.

One of the challenges facing on-site life cycles in densely settled areas is the limited energy generation potential and the limited filtration capacity per square foot of land area. Research on biomimicry (discussed in chapter 7) may give us blueprints for creating local and intensive ecosystems that increase waste absorption and create useful biomass or energy outputs. The idea of not just consuming and disposing, but actually *regenerating*, is a critical component in the development of successful and sustainable on-site life cycles.

HOW WE CAN FOSTER ON-SITE LIFE CYCLES

STRATEGY #8: Foster on-site life cycles at the building, campus, and neighborhood levels for water and energy; they offer great potential for economically reducing CO_2 in the built environment. Remove regulatory obstacles and modify existing frameworks that are preventing these technologies from becoming mainstream.

Federal Government

Revise utility regulation to encourage utilities to support on-site life cycles.

....

On-site life cycles could be encouraged through a utility regulation overhaul. As discussed in chapter 2, the current focus on predictability and planning within utilities often makes them reluctant to support innovation that might impact their traditional models for predicting demand. For instance, if a water utility upgrades its sewage mains and builds a treatment plant predicated on expected population growth in a region, it will tend to want to use that capacity in a predictable way as the population grows. On-site life cycles reduce customer demand for sewage treatment capacity; if they are widely adopted within a region they could delay capacity utilization of the new mains and treatment plant, causing the utility to fall short on its revenue growth projections.

Create more flexibility in how utilities finance capital investments and in how they price the services they sell to their customers.

....

Energy and water infrastructure projects tend to ratchet up capacity in large increments. To pay off the bonds used to finance these large projects, utilities are incented to "bill out" all the extra capacity as quickly as possible. This works at counter purposes to energy and water conservation efforts. This challenge is particularly evident as developers implement LEED for Neighborhood Development and Living Building Challenge projects that include small-scale power generation and on-site life cycles for water treatment. A utility that needs to make payments on its bonds has little incentive to support development proposals that would generate energy on-site, create a district scale utility to reuse waste heat, or capture, treat, and reuse water on-site; such projects would limit demands for the utility's centralized capacity. This is ironic, because decentralized energy and water systems can help offset the needs of a growing population, allowing the utility to go much longer before requiring another major capital investment. These types of issues will need to be resolved if innovative projects are to have a chance in the market.

It would undoubtedly be possible (and still profitable for lenders) for a utility and its financial institutions to structure a loan with a longer payback period to reduce the immediate pressure on the utility to use up new capacity. Unfortunately this would also result in increased carrying costs for the project, assuming the borrowing instrument was fixed-term bonds. But there is certainly a middle ground where the utility and the financial institutions could structure bonds that would provide an option to the utility to extend the term where this was deemed to be beneficial. At the time when opportunities arose for the utility to increase the life of the existing facility by supporting projects that reduced demand, the utility could make the trade-off between the benefit of delaying construction of the next increment of capacity versus the increased carrying cost of exercising the option to extend the bond term. It would be even more effective, however, to change the way that capacity is planned and delivered in the first place. Utilities need to strive for ways to grow and make capital investments much more incrementally than in the past, to reduce capital cost bubbles and allow room for innovation to help reduce demand.

Implement flexible pricing schemes that reward users for reducing demand during peaks.

More flexible pricing approaches offer another avenue for improved efficiency for utilities. Other types of service providers already use flexible delivery and pricing models. Internet service providers (ISPs) figured out early on that they didn't need to guarantee the same service level to all of their users and that implementing different service levels with different pricing could allow them to leverage their network more efficiently. Flexibility about service delivery, in the form of multitier service level agreements (SLAs), differential pricing for power consumed during peak and off-peak load times, and user transparency into load levels are all tools that are not easily available to utilities under current regulation. Such tools could significantly transform the ability of utilities to use the current power supply efficiently and leverage new clean sources of power, such as wind and solar, that don't produce continuous-level supply.

As journalist Kate Galbraith recently reported in the *New York Times*, Idaho Power has taken some very positive steps in the right direction.[13] Since 2004, Idaho Power has been offering its customers cash incentives to reduce energy usage during crucial peak load times. Participating farmers make the biggest dent by agreeing to turn off their electric irrigation pumps for as many as fifteen hours a month during the summer. Although they take on some risk of crop damage, they reap savings of as much as 30 percent or more on energy expenses. Individual households can participate in similar programs, earning cash for insulating their attics or allowing the utility to switch home air-conditioners off for short intermittent periods during peak demand. The program has allowed Idaho Power to build new power plants at a far slower pace than the rapidly growing population would have otherwise required. It has also changed the state's political environment to favor energy efficiency.

Allow users of local renewable energy infrastructure to earn clean energy credits.

Governments currently provide a wide variety of renewable energy credits to buildings that implement various forms of "green" energy, such as the installation of solar panels. But in many cases, if the building acquires its energy from a third-party local renewable source, it is not eligible for these credits. These schemes should be restructured to ensure that a building that connects to local renewable energy infrastructure receives the same credits as if the renewable energy capability was established within the building itself.

State and Local Governments

Alter building codes to allow for local generation and disposal as well as water use in series.

Building codes set baseline standards for quality and safety. Much of the water and energy parts of the code were originally created in an era when these goals were best served through centralized systems. Since then, technology has evolved. Policy makers now understand that parallel localized systems for energy and water can reduce environmental impact and sometimes even improve service levels by alleviating shortages. But most codes, as they currently exist, don't contemplate a balance between two modes of generation or parallel systems of pipes. Regulations that create this flexibility would reduce barriers to adoption. Standards for drinking and cooking water must remain high, for example, and electrical equipment needs to meet safety standards. But a code with provisions that supported grey water or rainwater capture as well as water treatment would pave the way for developers, redevelopers, and contractors to implement many solutions using existing technologies without the costly burden of proof each time. In establishing the code changes necessary to foster implementation of these relatively new and still evolving technologies, regulators should consider results-oriented frameworks as discussed in chapter 2.

Create local improvement districts (LIDs) to finance on-site life cycle projects.

State and local governments can support neighborhood-level life cycles by supporting the creation of local improvement districts (LIDs) for energy and water life cycle infrastructure. LIDs are financing vehicles that allow residents of a small defined area, such as a block or a street, to issue bonds backed by the city or state to fund infrastructure projects. The small area agrees to be taxed at a higher rate to repay the investment over time, and the government-backed financing results in a low interest rate, making the projects more affordable (and more competitive with the utilites' cost of borrowing). To this point, LIDs have been primarily used for community projects like road improvements or streetcar capital investments—extending them to cover small-scale generation or waste treatment plants would be a new and enabling step for many states and municipalities.

Local government nervousness about supporting the financing of systems they don't understand well will be a significant challenge in establishing successful LIDs for neighborhood life cycles. Utilities, however, have considerable experience in operating these types of systems and in analyzing and predicting demand. They are in a much better position to make informed lending decisions. To foster innovation, local governments should look for ways to encourage their utilities to support the financing of energy and water LIDs; this approach would also lead to inherent coordination between utilities' "primary" systems and the development of district-level life cycle systems.

Ensure that local zoning does not create barriers to inter- or intra-block resource sharing. Encourage pilot projects.

To be most effective, LIDs should be coupled with a revision of zoning provisions, which in many areas prevent multiple buildings or multiple owners from tapping into private small-scale utility infrastructure. Although much of the technology that can be applied to campus- or neighborhood-level generation or treatment is maturing, standards with respect to how the infrastructure is owned, how capacity is shared, how quality is maintained, and how ownership is transferred are still relatively untested. States and municipalities could support the development of infrastructure by supporting multiple pilot projects, monitoring performance, and supporting the development of standard operating agreements.

In addition to supporting innovation, pilot projects provide a basis for regulatory evolution. New technologies and system designs tend to be unpalatable to risk-averse governments, because their success is never guaranteed. Because on-site life cycles are still in an innovative stage, however, overregulation before we know what works and what doesn't will stop progress in its tracks. One way to mitigate this tension is to permit entrepreneurial individuals to use innovative strategies on the condition that they report their performance later, so that the tests can serve as pilot projects. In general, good reporting structures have the potential to increase the comfort of state and local governments with testing new technologies or new forms of governance supporting critical infrastructure. Good reporting can also reduce concerns about health and life safety risks around new infrastructure and allows governments to leverage the knowledge generated from pilot projects.

It is, of course, essential that good oversight and management remain in place to ensure that decentralized water supplies are clean and safe. One option for achieving this goal is to offer building owners the option to purchase a monitoring or even a maintenance service for an on-site life cycle system from a public utility. This approach might make regulators more comfortable, and utilities might agree since they have the opportunity to be involved and make at least some profit. Such arrangements would probably require new legal mechanisms to the limit the utility's liability, and even then some public utilities may feel too uncomfortable about maintaining private systems on private land to offer such a service.

At the level of the property owner, liability management is arguably even more important. People and companies that agree to test out new systems should receive an appropriate amount of protection, because there currently is no standard for code compliance to serve as a shield. One option may be to look abroad for standards already being used in places like the state of Victoria, Australia. In Victoria, which faces significant water shortages, the local authorities have recognized the need to set a regional goal for reducing household use of drinking water through strategies like recycling and reusing rainwater and grey water. The Department of Human Services and the Department of Sustainability and Environment have established a set of statewide guidelines that encourage the use of these on-site systems within a framework that takes precautions to ensure health, quality, and safe use of alternative water supplies.[14]

Developers and Investors

Stay tuned to the evolution of technology. Develop expertise and make a point to be at the table as new tools, strategies, and policies for on-site life cycles evolve.

Although on-site life cycle technology may seem to be some distance from mainstream adoption, consumers are increasingly interested in these systems because of their reduced environmental impact and potential for long-term cost-effectiveness. Developers may be cautious about answering this demand from the market until the regulatory environment makes it possible to do so with adequately managed risk. Although code changes that encourage on-site life cycles will not happen overnight, developers and investors need to stay informed about the technologies and policies affecting their implementation. It is highly likely that consumer demand will cause code structures to become more supportive quite rapidly, and the developers who have the expertise to exploit on-site life cycle solutions will be the most successful in the new market.

LIFE CYCLES IN A NUTSHELL

On-site life cycles for water and energy employ new technologies; they are only sparsely used in the United States, and the current regulatory framework discourages their implementation. However, they offer very significant potential for reducing the carbon footprint of the built environment. Governments should be proactive in creating the regulatory flexibility required to encourage rather than discourage their introduction. Developers, in turn, must become much more knowledgeable about these technologies in order to capitalize on them as they become viable.

CHAPTER 9

REGIONAL TRANSPORTATION

*If you listened to Americans talk about their governments' responsibility
to provide roads for their cars, you might think they were all socialists.*

—AL HURD

Transportation is a response to the need people have for access to places
and things that they can't get to on foot. Because transportation creates value by providing access, by definition transportation networks
are useful to the extent that they effectively connect people with the
things they need. Assuming people have many needs that can't be met within
walking distance of their homes, they require roads, vehicles, and transit to get
to and between places. The notion of transportation networks is an important
one, because if a means of transportation doesn't meet most of the mobility
needs of individuals, it won't get used. A light rail line in a vacuum that connects only two points is practically useless unless everybody lives at one end
and only needs to go to the other end. The light rail line creates more value
if it has park-and-rides at both ends. It can then get people from many points
to one point, but it still can't get people from many points to many points. If
we add plentiful connections to bus routes at both ends of the light rail line,
it begins to have a substantial network effect that can provide value to many
people with many different access needs.

Over the past century or so, most of our lives have become regional; we spend the bulk of our time in the vicinity of our home city (often referred to as a metropolitan area). Almost 80 percent of U.S. residents and 50 percent of the world's population now live in urban areas where they work within the surrounding region, join regional clubs or teams, watch the games of a regional sports team, and recreate and shop at amenities and stores within the region.[1] Because of this, a high percentage of access needs can be satisfied at a regional level. Unfortunately, access solutions that interconnect only parts of the region tend to satisfy only some of the people only some of the time.

Chapter 6 looked at ways to support the development of self-sufficient neighborhoods that would have the effect of shortening some individual daily trips or eliminating them entirely. Naturally, designing the built environment to simultaneously reduce the need for vehicles, infrastructure, fuel, and trips in the first place is the most helpful action we can take. This chapter examines how development patterns and transportation networks can reduce the carbon intensity of the trips that must continue to exist. A 2009 Urban Land Institute report concludes that transportation greenhouse gas (GHG) emissions are the result of the interaction of four factors: vehicle fuel efficiency, the carbon content of the fuel burned, the number of miles that vehicles travel, and the operational efficiency experienced during travel. The report summarizes the four basic strategies that can be used to reduce GHGs as follows:

» Vehicle Technology—Improving the energy efficiency of the vehicle fleet by implementing more advanced technologies

» Fuel Technology—Reducing the carbon content of fuels through the use of alternative fuels (for instance, natural gas, biofuels, and hydrogen)

» Travel Activity—Reducing the number of miles traveled by transportation vehicles, or shifting those miles to more efficient modes of transportation

» Vehicle and System Operations—Improving the efficiency of the transportation network so that a larger share of vehicle operations occur in favorable conditions, with respect to speed and smoothness of traffic flow, resulting in more fuel efficient vehicle operations.[2]

What would a less carbon-intensive transportation map look like? First, it would account for more people per motorized vehicle. Larger vehicles operating at capacity have a much lower carbon impact and a lower economic cost per passenger-mile traveled than vehicles driven by a single occupant. To put a group of people into one vehicle, however, those people must live or work close to a common starting point and be able to meet many of their needs at a common end point. Clearly, then, encouraging compact, mixed-use neighborhood development concentrated in urban centers is a strong enabler of a more carbon-efficient transportation system. But the reality is that that the majority of existing development patterns are relatively low density. We must therefore focus on how we can optimize the time, cost, and carbon impact of travel within existing and evolving patterns in an entire region.

Systems theory deals with the interplay of local and global optimization. Most systems have both local optima (solutions that best serve one portion of the system) and global optima (the best solutions to problems when the entire system is considered). Not surprisingly, the two are often not the same. When only one part of the solution set is examined, we may find a local optimum, but the best solution for the most players, the global optimum, comes from looking at all the possibilities in the broadest way. Transportation networks are no exception to this rule. On the one hand, if we manage the network through separate pools of funds for different modes of transportation, each pool of funds (or mode) tends to find its own optimal balance, or local optimum solution. On the other hand, if we create one pool of funds that is managed across all modes together to meet all the mobility needs within the region, we also create the possibility of reaching a more economically efficient optimum, and likely a more carbon efficient one too.

How does this manifest in concrete terms? In the United States public transit systems are often funded at the municipal or county level; because major metropolitan areas encompass several counties among which people regularly travel, subregional optimization is sadly the norm rather than the exception. Multiple public transportation authorities have different funding sources, and they serve different customers and neighborhoods. In this scenario it's easy to understand how different organizations with different mandates might do well in one portion of the region, or for one customer base, but provide suboptimal service in aggregate to meet overall regional needs. While local services often do make attempts to act in a coordinated fashion, their funding structures require that their first priority be service to their particular constituency, rather than development of an optimal network solution for the region.

In 1999 Gerald Frug, the Louis D. Brandeis Professor of Law at Harvard Law School and a leading academic authority on local government law, published the influential book *City Making*. This work is devoted to discussing the dynamic that causes adjacent cities within the same metropolitan area to act in their own narrow self-interest to the detriment of their region as a whole. Frug makes the point that although the fates of individual cities and suburbs within a region are "inextricably entangled," the legal system has developed a tradition of allowing each suburb to behave with absolutely no regard for the well-being of its neighbors.[3] No other legal entity in society, not even a private sector corporation or an individual, is so unfettered by responsibility to act to some degree in ways that do not harm its community. To help correct this lack of balance, Frug argues that the legal system should weigh any use of public funds by cities in terms of its impact on and benefit to the city's region as a whole.

Segregation of budgets also undermines regional transportation solutions. Even though well-used public transit is almost always the most efficient means of moving people long distances, private vehicles also play an important part in regional mobility. Safe and well-maintained roads are critical to regional transportation networks. However, their capital sources are completely separate from transit capital sources, and within roads, capital budgets are further compartmentalized by specific use. Because roads and transit are part of the same mobility network, the separation of road and transit capital budgets tends to create barriers to achieving economically efficient and carbon-efficient transportation networks.

Frameworks that aggregate mobility budgets on a regional basis and strive to maximize access would deliver the most value for the lowest cost, and at a lower carbon footprint. Metrics that support this type of analysis might include:

» Energy consumed per passenger mile traveled.
» People moved per mile of road.
» Percentage of access needs satisfied per dollar spent on transportation/transit.
» Overall person-miles traveled in the region (with a goal for people to meet all their needs without wasting time and money traveling).
» Time-efficiency of bundled trips as compared to single-occupancy vehicle (SOV) trips.
» Carbon-intensiveness of miles traveled (SOV trips versus bundled trips).

Mobility is increased in two ways. As a first step, we can add capacity incrementally by increasing the number of vehicles on the roads and rails, but after a point capacity becomes constrained by infrastructure limitations. The second step, expanding the infrastructure, usually entails large up-front costs and substantial carbon impacts, as well as new ongoing operating costs. Chapter 8 discussed how on-site life cycles can avoid the carbon impact of infrastructure expansion projects by finding ways to reduce pressure on existing facilities. A similar approach can be applied to transportation networks through improvements in trip bundling that provide real mobility value and have the effect of freeing up transportation network capacity.

It must be noted that the fundamental inefficiency in trip bundling is lost time. Bundling trips (whether by public transit, carpool, or shuttle) typically adds time to the trip in the form of routing (riders going to or from a transfer point and waiting for the vehicle) and in grouping trips (drivers waiting for critical mass and stopping to let riders off and on). People typically make a behavioral switch to using transit or carpools when the cost of SOV travel gets too high and, even more, when the bundled trip becomes time-competitive with SOV travel (often due to congestion slowing down the SOV). Regional mobility solutions must therefore take into account the need to make transit more time-competitive and in turn more likely to attract new riders.

RECOGNIZING EFFECTIVE REGIONAL TRANSPORTATION

New York City has five geographically delineated boroughs, nearly all of which are separated by water. The populations of the boroughs are widely diverse, the histories and land uses are disparate, and the settlement densities vary widely. Nonetheless, the boroughs have long been administered under the umbrella of one regional government: New York City. This has enabled efficiency in administration, global optimum solutions to many challenges, and a mobility system that is second to none in this country, providing residents of the boroughs with a multitude of access opportunities. Bus service is planned and delivered by the same agency that runs the subway and many of the ferries. The fare system is harmonized, and the network measures its success in terms of overall ridership and trip time, rather than competing for mode split or fastest ridership on any one mode. It is such a strong network, and provides access to such a high ratio of daily destinations, that about half the households in New York City (not just in Manhattan) choose to not own a car at all, versus 8 percent nationally.[4]

New York City, however, stands alone in the United States in its high use of public transit, perhaps because of its history, its density, and the time-competitiveness of using transit instead of a car in the city. All other American cities have a significantly higher percentage of SOV trips, and most are

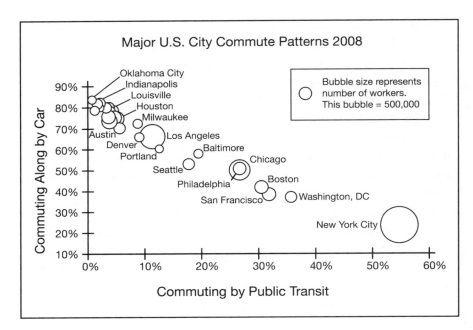

9.1. Commute patterns for major U.S. cities. Source: Arturo Ramos, Wikimedia Commons

dramatically higher (see figure 9.1).[5] It should be noted that the results shown in figure 9.1 would almost certainly be skewed even more highly toward SOV commuting if the metropolitan areas, not just the central cities, were graphed. It is clear that, outside of a few large cities like New York City, Washington, D.C., San Francisco, and Boston, we still have a very long way to go before transit becomes a major mode of transportation in most U.S. cities.

Some American cities, however, like Portland, Oregon, are making very impressive efforts to make public transit an attractive and frequent choice for travelers in the city. The city of Portland has a population of about 580,000, and the metropolitan area contains about 2.6 million citizens.[6] This makes it typical of many larger cities in the United States. Portland provides coordinated bus and rail service on a regional basis through a multicounty transportation authority. It manages investment of the metropolitan area's share of federal tax dollars over multiple modes of transportation rather than in separate pools. Through its transportation master plan, Portland ensures that services dovetail across all components of the transit system, including buses, rail, streetcars, and even an aerial tram. All regions of the city have good access to the city core on one of its four light-rail lines. The result is that Portland's rate of public transit use rivals that of much larger cities in the United States and is higher than in most similarly sized cities.[7]

State and local governments bear most of the responsibility for regional infrastructure that moves not only people but also freight and other goods. Trade efficiency is a fundamental underpinning of regional economic competitiveness: road and rail networks need to be up to the challenge. When road networks came into the purview of governments—as part of the public good, enabling efficient economies—there was an underlying assumption that people wouldn't use more road capacity than they needed. People aren't going to drive around for nothing, so the thinking went. But in a land-constrained world, free roads can actually amount to using public dollars to subsidize sprawl. If we live within walking distance of work, we use no road capacity to get there in contrast to someone who lives an hour's drive away. The person who lives an hour away so that he or she can have two acres of backyard is creating an economic burden that we all pay for with our tax dollars. Clearly we can't all live on the head of a pin. We need roads, and many people live further away from services and places of work out of necessity. But by the same token, we would do well to reexamine our system of "free" roads, which allocates limited capacity in a way that is not conducive to economic productivity.

A carbon tax will get us some of the way there by increasing the cost of driving and getting our economy to squeeze more economic productivity (and carbon efficiency) into every driving mile. But a carbon tax doesn't address the fact that not all our infrastructure is capacity constrained to the same degree. Pay-to-use private highways have gained traction in some parts of the United States and allow for the allocation of efficient infrastructure to the most productive uses. Dedicated highway lanes for buses or carpools have the benefit of making transit time-competitive with single-occupancy vehicle (SOV) travel and increasing the efficiency of our infrastructure for moving people. Dedicating a lane to carpools and buses may at first seem like a loss of capacity, but it actually enables the highway to move more *people* per lane-mile. Dedicated lanes for high-occupancy vehicles (HOV) improve our infrastructure capacity *and* our carbon efficiency at the same time.

HOW WE CAN IMPROVE REGIONAL TRANSPORTATION

STRATEGY #9: Plan and manage transportation systems on a regional basis (versus municipal or state level) because the vast majority of mobility requirements are regional. Coordinate regional investments in transportation infrastructure to optimize the mobility of individuals and goods rather than the mobility of cars.

Federal and State Governments

Allocate road capacity in a way that maximizes person-trip efficiency.

If you travel by bus or carpool, you use less road capacity per person than someone driving alone. In exchange, you may get a little lower-cost ride but nothing else. No time improvement, no tax break for your reduced usage of expensive infrastructure. HOV lanes are a step in the right direction, because they provide a compensating time benefit to people who invest time in grouping trips. HOV lanes have been implemented in many U.S. cities, and the state of Virginia even converts a ten-mile section of I-66 near Washington, D.C., to HOV-only use during rush hour.[8]

In many places, however, HOV lanes have become congested and no longer provide much of a time advantage. There has been fierce resistance from organizations such as the National Motorists Association to converting more lanes to HOV because travel times for SOV drivers usually increase further as a result.[9] In other quarters there is debate about whether to make HOV lanes open to buses only or to continue extending the benefit to carpools of just three-plus or only two-plus travelers. In chapter 10 we talk in some detail about the city of Bogotá, Colombia, which has taken the step of dedicating HOV lanes to buses only, with officials arguing that this measure provides the only viable balance between local economic realities and the mobility needs of city residents.

One way to deal with these issues is to allocate road capacity on a per-person-trip basis. Many state and interstate roads already have electronic signage in urban areas to update drivers on travel times, road conditions, detours, or accidents. Cities like Houston, San Diego, and Montreal even use these types of signs to reverse the direction of travel in certain lanes during rush hours.[10] This same form of signage could be used to dynamically allocate road capacity. If an HOV lane allowing two-plus carpools is approaching its maximum capacity, then each person in that lane is using half (or less) of the road capacity than the SOV lanes. At that point it makes sense to switch another lane from SOV to HOV so that riders who have bundled their trips get their due capacity. One further refinement might be that the newly converted lane is three-plus. If the second HOV lane fills to the point where it is carrying the same number of cars as the SOV lanes, then a third HOV lane should be added.

A related approach that has worked well in many cities is to run passenger rail service along major highways that are prone to congestion. The routing not only supports existing commute patterns but also gives people sitting in their cars in traffic an obvious and explicit reminder of the option to move to a more time-efficient mode.

Change transportation funding from mode-oriented to mobility-oriented.

Federal and state governments provide money to regions and cities for construction and operation of transportation infrastructure, and those funds are almost universally allocated in separately designated pools for roads and transit. Both levels of government could send a clearer signal in favor of regional mobility planning by collaborating to bundle road and transit capital and operational funds, and by prioritizing funding to agencies that plan networks and manage implementation at a regional level. This in turn would incent counties and municipalities to group their budgets and invest in a regional body with administration and planning authority.

Some of the flaws in the current funding structure are summarized very well in *Growing Cooler: The Evidence on Urban Development and Climate Change*, a book published in 2007 by the Urban Land Institute. Among the biggest barriers to aligning transportation goals at a regional level are:

» *Lack of performance-based standards.* The evaluation criteria for assigning federal dollars to states for transportation projects focuses on planning and process, not on results. Goals and standards for transportation established at a national level (and ideally based on a long-term vision for climate stability) would allow more accurate evaluation of state efforts.[11]

» *Funding policies that reward vehicle miles traveled (VMT) growth rather than improving mobility.* Traditionally, the federal government has awarded transportation dollars to states proportionately based on how much the citizens of that state are driving. Increases in VMT also drive up state revenues from gas taxes that are used to fund roads. These policies currently align to encourage VMT growth (creating a self-reinforcing system), rather than encouraging mobility solutions that temper greenhouse gas emissions.[12]

» *Funding policies that favor new highway construction and expansion.* State transit projects typically receive 50 percent federal financing, while highway capacity-building projects frequently receive 80 to 90 percent financing. In addition, transit projects face a more competitive review process and intense ongoing federal oversight, while highway projects generally do not.[13]

» *States don't allocate adequate funding to metropolitan planning organizations (MPOs).* Because the federal government allows state governments to choose how much funding is allocated to MPOs for comprehensive regional transportation solutions, MPOs often receive only a tiny portion relative to what they need. If a regional transportation solution is to serve the national transportation goals in the best way possible, federal funding should go directly to the MPO responsible for implementation.[14]

Consider embodied carbon as part of the impact of infrastructure projects.

Finally, to the extent that governments engage in providing transportation infrastructure that serves the public good, they should evaluate projects based on how much access is created and the life cycle carbon footprint (embodied and operational) of the infrastructure. This is an important point because some modes of transportation have very low operational emissions but very significant up-front carbon impacts (e.g., rail tunnels).

Local Governments

Aggregate mobility funding and decision making in a single regional body.

Many of the strategies described for state and federal jurisdictions earlier in this chapter are also relevant to local government. In particular, local governments could serve their regions better by aggregating funds for mobility improvements and investing in a regional body with planning and budget authority. Here are a few more ideas that are particularly relevant at the local level.

Make street parking subject to the laws of supply and demand.

In nearly all large cities, street parking is notoriously difficult to find at busy times of the day. One study conducted in New York City in 2007 found that 45 percent of the traffic in the study area in Brooklyn was caused by drivers looking for parking spots.[15] Regardless of the exact percentage of "hunting" drivers in any given city, there can be little doubt that at busy times of the day, the scarcity of parking is a significant cause of carbon emissions and other forms of pollution.

To deal with this issue, San Francisco implemented a trial in 2008 where they converted 25 percent of parking spaces to a dynamic demand-pricing scheme so that at peak times of the day, meter prices would be high enough to ensure that there was always some parking available. Prices were lowered during off-peak hours to a level that would keep most parking spots earning revenue. Other innovations, such as allowing motorists to add money to their meters by phone and easing time limits during off hours, were further concessions to market forces.[16] These types of strategies alleviate some of the market distortions (and hidden subsidies of cars) caused by underpriced street parking. They also reduce carbon emissions both directly (fewer cars cruising for parking) and indirectly (fewer cars trying to use the streets in the first place because drivers are unwilling to pay market price for parking).

Consider congestion pricing for areas with an overloaded road infrastructure.

"Congestion pricing" is the name given to a scheme for charging vehicles a fee for the use of the roads in particularly busy parts of cities. The most notable implementation of congestion pricing has been in effect in London since 2002, when a charge (now eight pounds, or about thirteen dollars) was assessed on all vehicles entering the congestion zone (with some exceptions for buses, taxis, and minibuses over a certain size). A number of other cities have similar systems, including Singapore, Rome, and Milan. Three cities in Norway have implemented related schemes in the form of road tolls for city centers.[17] An attempt by New York City mayor Michael Bloomberg to implement congestion pricing in 2008 died in the state legislature (a reminder that some aspects of this strategy may not be totally within the control of cities).

The theoretical advantage of these approaches is that they put a price on the use of valuable infrastructure, thereby bringing market forces into play. Either congestion is reduced because the price is not worth the value received by a driver, or the city raises extra revenue for additional infrastructure or transit. It's important to note that congestion pricing can only work well in regions with good transit service. After all, you can't incent people to switch modes when there is nothing to switch *to*. Critics of congestion pricing argue that it is expensive to administer, and it does not really reduce congestion in any case. The London implementation has been studied exhaustively, but obtaining uncontestable results is next to impossible because of the number of variables at play over time (e.g., changes to the road network and the effect of road works). Data presented by the city of London indicate that four years after the scheme was implemented, traffic in the congestion zone had dropped by 16 percent, travel times were reduced by about 20 percent, and, not surprisingly, emissions of CO_2 and other pollutants were down significantly as well.

As the New York experience attests, however, congestion pricing is not a popular concept in the United States (or anywhere else, for that matter). Despite its political challenges, though, the concept can be a potent tool in reducing or delaying the need for (or funding of) new road infrastructure and in reducing congestion and carbon emissions in cities. For that reason local and state governments need to find ways to implement these schemes when the situation warrants it.

Consider strategies to improve acceptance of grouped transportation options.

Local governments should consider strategies to improve grouped transportation viability from a time and access point of view as a way to free up capacity on existing roads for freight or for trips that require roads. Since a significant determinant of what mode people use is force of habit, some cities in Central and South America as well as in Asia have had success in allowing only even- or odd-numbered license plates into the center city on certain days. Other governments have closed the center city to SOV cars one or two days a year to encourage people to give grouped trips or alternate modes a try.

Eliminate barriers to complementary trip-sharing modes.

Many municipalities cap the number of taxi licenses issued and ban paid ride-sharing and private minibus services. These measures (often implemented in the belief that they are required to foster a viable taxi service) limit service levels, discourage innovation, and generally penalize people who don't own cars. This type of market-distorting regulation is counterproductive to the public interest and should be eliminated.

Invest in infrastructure to support cycling as transportation.

In many cities in Europe and in other parts of the world, cycling is a very heavily used mode of transportation, yielding obvious infrastructure and carbon savings. If local governments in the United States want to encourage more residents to bike as regular means of transportation, they must allocate transportation funds for the street-level infrastructure improvements needed to make cycling a safe and viable option. An Oregon state legislature bill enacted in 1971 requires cities and counties to spend reasonable amounts of the state highway funds they receive on facilities for pedestrians and cyclists. The bill mandates those funds be used exclusively for improvements along public streets open to motor vehicles.[18]

As a result of this consistent dedicated government funding, the city of Portland now boasts a variety of innovative roadway treatments, including "bike boxes" that give cyclists a designated, visible space to wait at busy intersections, "buffered" or "enhanced" bike lanes, and wide paths that allow "shy zones" on either side to further separate cyclists from moving and parked vehicles. According to American Community Survey data, 6.4 percent of Portlanders reported biking to work in 2008.[19] This puts Portland first in bike commuting among America's thirty largest cities. As impressive as Portland's statistics are, however, a look at the city of Amsterdam, where residents take more daily trips by bicycle than by automobile, shows what can really be accomplished when cycling becomes an integral part of the regional culture and transportation system.[20]

To the extent that geography allows cycling to be a viable option for a substantial portion of the population, bicycle trips can eliminate many local car trips from roads as well as free up capacity. Well-known photographs taken in Muenster, Germany, graphically illustrate the differences in road space consumed by the same group of people when traveling by car or by bicycle (see fig. 9.2).

A significant mode shift to bicycles requires its own infrastructure, although it is not nearly as costly or intensive as infrastructure for motorized modes. First and foremost, bicyclists need safe places to ride. Dedicated bicycle lanes are helpful, but many cities site them in the door-opening zone for parallel parked cars, which poses a substantial hazard. Dedicated bike paths or lanes inboard of the sidewalk edge are much safer. In addition, regulation such as Amsterdam's, which imposes stiff penalties on drivers who drive aggressively and endanger cyclists, can do a great deal to improve road safety for urban cyclists. Second, bicycle travel requires plentiful, adequate, and safe places to lock bicycles. Parking options can range from the standard on-sidewalk racks found in most U.S. cities to more complex solutions, like the mechanical bike storage devices found in extremely dense cities like Tokyo.[21] Recently the Northwest cities of Portland and Seattle have replaced some car-parking spots with on-street "bike corrals" in neighborhoods where cycling

9.2. Road space required to transport the same number of people by car and by bicycle. Source: City of Muenster, Germany

and walking are a more common form of transportation. Building standards and codes that incent the provision of lockers, showering, and bicycle storage facilities provide the framework for significant increases in bicycle ridership year round, even in areas with a few months of inclement weather.

Developers and Other Private Companies

Unbundle parking from rental rates and let the market decide how much is needed.

Parking provides a good example of where changing frameworks can make the market more efficient, make the enterprise more profitable, and reduce carbon emissions. As cities have become denser and close-in land prices have risen, providing parking within a parking garage or building (referred to as structured parking) has become more cost efficient than surface parking in many places. However, a minimum amount of structured parking is often required by cities, and it is expensive to build. As a rule of thumb in many markets in the United States, it costs about twenty-five thousand dollars per stall in an above-ground building. Below-grade parking comes with an even heftier price tag, averaging out at about forty thousand dollars per stall, depending on

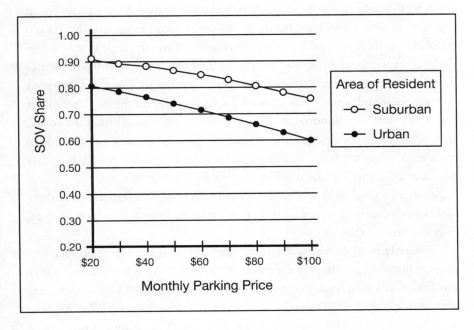

9.3. Effect of parking costs on use of single-occupancy vehicles (SOVs). Source: Transportation Research Board

variables such as soil type and garage depth. As a result, developers have been disinclined to build more structured parking than their tenants really need.

As a means of managing the transportation impacts of new development, many local and state governments require developers to create transportation demand management (TDM) plans as a precondition for obtaining a development permit. TDM plans can provide a means for building owners to creatively ensure that the demand for infrastructure and parking falls within the planned supply by offering subsidized or free transit passes to their employees and charging employees to park. As demonstrated in figure 9.3, paid parking substantially affects mode splits within urban and suburban environments that are served by transit.[22]

There are alternatives to requiring developers to build structured parking that could also foster improved public transit. Many developers would be delighted to be given the choice between contributing to a fund dedicated to local transit service improvements versus being forced to build a prescribed minimum of parking spaces. Cities would derive substantial benefit from such a scheme so both parties would benefit. In locations where cities do not enforce minimum parking capacity requirements, a transit capacity charge could be levied, coupled with a firm commitment to allocate any collected funds to local service. A portion of the project's impact fees or mitigation fees could be allocated to transit rather than to increasing road capacity. It is worth noting that some cities with strong public transportation systems have even established structured parking *maximums* rather than minimums.

Interestingly, when developers create leases for their tenants, the leases themselves typically include parking, either as a number of stalls provided per one thousand square feet of rented space, or as an add-on, typically at one hundred to two hundred dollars per month per space. What's really odd about this is that the developer (or owner) is subsidizing the tenant's parking spots with his or her base rent. Even if the tenant pays two hundred dollars per month for parking, the resulting twenty-four hundred dollars per year is less than a 10 percent return on the cost of providing that structured parking spot. Development projects offering returns lower than 10 percent are typically not financeable.

The only possible reason that developers are using rental models that subsidize structured parking for their tenants is that they've been doing it that way for a really long time. In many cases they probably don't realize that there are other options. The research isn't rigorous, but we've posed the question to many developers and commercial real estate brokers: Why not just let the market decide how much parking it needs and be transparent about the cost? The question has been met only with the answer of tradition. Just as government can benefit from rethinking some basic frameworks and standards, so too can the business world, to its own profit.

As one indication of how behaviors can change under the right circumstances, TDM plans, once loathsome to developers, have actually earned some respect. Originally seen as a penalty imposed by the government, TDM programs allow companies to provide what many employees now see as a perk—a free or subsidized transit pass—and can allow building owners to save money if the TDM effectively allows them to construct less parking than building codes would otherwise require.[23]

Offer complementary transit service that makes transit viable for employees.

In many regions the existing transportation network for both roads and transit is radially organized, with many major routes extending out from a central destination, like the spokes on a bicycle wheel. This makes it efficient to take trips from the center to the periphery, but the radial organization leaves large sections of unserved areas in between the spokes, which get larger and larger as you travel farther from the central hub. When home-work-home commutes are considered as a significant portion of total trips taken in a region, transit affords a competitive commuting option only to employees who live on a spoke and work in the center.

Employers located farther out on the spokes, however, tend to have a much more difficult time bringing in their employees by transit. To compete for the best employees, these companies need to provide a substantial amount of free parking, often at a hefty cost. In some parts of the country large regional employers with facilities grouped away from the center have begun to offer their own transit service. In Seattle the University of Washington and some of its affiliated Health Science Research Institutes operate a private shuttle service linking residential neighborhoods and the different research campuses. An even more striking example is the Microsoft approach, introduced in chapter 4. In 2007, Microsoft employed nearly fifty thousand people in the Puget Sound area, most of them at the Redmond headquarters on the east side of Lake Washington. Much of the company's relatively youthful employment base lives on the west side of the lake, attracted by the more hip urban vibe of Seattle. Many employees therefore face a long commute.

The existing radial Metro bus service does not connect Seattle's residential neighborhoods with the Microsoft campus in an efficient way. As a result, Microsoft was not only bearing substantial real estate costs to provide parking, but it was losing human capital to competitors who were located closer to where the workforce lived. The Redmond campus is too big to move, so Microsoft did the next best thing. The company created a shuttle service called the Connector that offers direct service between each residential neighborhood in Seattle and the Redmond campus. The buses are comfortable, have wireless Internet, are highly time-competitive with car travel, free up productive time for employees, and have been so successful that they often book up online twenty-four hours in advance. Microsoft's response to providing a regional transit solution has encouraged employee retention while lowering real estate parking requirements. With structured parking costing up to forty thousand dollars per stall, that's a dramatic cost savings.

While not every company can achieve this economy of scale, consider the example of McKinstry, a Northwest mechanical and energy services contractor. Located in a southern industrial neighborhood of Seattle, where transit service is relatively poor, the company had difficulty increasing transit ridership among its employees. Complicating things, many of its middle-income employees commuted from suburbs that were several miles north or south of downtown. In a creative compromise, McKinstry encourages employees to commute to a south-central rail and bus hub by paying for their transit passes and providing direct shuttle service from the station to the office at frequent intervals in the morning and afternoon.

Support telecommuting for knowledge workers.

Employers can contribute to freeing up regional infrastructure capacity by allowing employees to telecommute. An individual working even one day a week from home can reduce his or her regional capacity consumed by 20 percent, benefiting the region as a whole. By providing access without mobility requirements, employers can eliminate at least two trips from the regional daily trip map.

When possible, invest in building-level improvements that complement neighborhood infrastructure.

The built environment can support low-emissions transportation even at the individual building level. Although street-level improvements like bike boxes and buffered lanes are in the hands of the local government, developers can play a major role in making cycling a viable transportation choice for their tenants. By installing secure indoor bike racks and shower facilities, building owners can alleviate some of the most common annoyances that prevent employees from commuting by bike. These improvements are a relatively small investment, compared to even a handful of extra parking stalls.

Environmental Nonprofits and Educational Institutions

Provide models for cost savings of regional transportation solutions.

Universities and think tanks can provide valuable resources to governments contemplating new metrics for mobility or trying to understand the economic impacts of regionally optimized transportation funding. Because transportation funding is complex, entrenched, and highly politicized, it is one of the hardest areas in which to create pilot projects (which we have advocated in other chapters). In the absence of being able to test new strategies on the *real* system (as in the case of pilot projects), models of the system have a critically important role in understanding how proposed changes will play out.

Governments contemplating some of the changes described in this chapter are hungry for information about their consequences. Advocates of regional transportation could benefit from data and models that show the value of global optimization. As an example, the Brookings Institution has been very focused on this issue. In particular, a number of works by the urban land strategist and developer Christopher Leinberger of the Brookings Institution look at the characteristics of successful regional transit systems and funding structures and the interplay of these systems with the economic ecosystems that develop around transit nodes.

REGIONAL TRANSPORTATION IN A NUTSHELL

Urban mobility requirements drive a major component of our daily CO_2 emissions. Meeting these requirements using HOVs or bicycles can significantly reduce costs and carbon generation. In most U.S. cities SOVs are the overwhelmingly dominant mode of transportation, primarily because over the past hundred years we have focused on providing roads for cars rather than broadly optimizing regional transportation solutions. We can meet urban mobility needs with lower carbon impact if governments support all modes of transportation as a single system interconnected for regional mobility. Focusing on systemwide economics with pricing transparency will tend to drive infrastructure investment toward the most efficient mode split.

CHAPTER 10

DELIGHT

No problem can be solved from the same consciousness that created it. You must learn to see the world anew.

—ALBERT EINSTEIN

S uccessful product developers know that they create value by meeting customer requirements. People who develop consumer products use all sorts of tools, from focus groups to surveys to behavioral observation, to understand customer needs. But in many cases, customers' expectations are limited by what they already know. In the immortal words of Henry Ford: "If I'd asked people what they wanted, they'd have said faster horses."[1] The invention of the automobile at the end of the nineteenth century and Ford's determination to make it affordable to "the great multitude" by introducing the Model T in 1909 forever changed the world. Solutions that are world changing, that fundamentally alter people's behaviors and perceptions of value, are often so far beyond the realm of previous experience that before their creation they were unimaginable by most of us. The solutions that reach wide-scale adoption are those that not only deliver the basic explicit components of value but also delight customers beyond their expectations.

Halting climate change will demand a massive shift in behavior. It will require changes in patterns of settlement and mobility, and perhaps even adjustments in the perceived value of many of the goods, services, and interactions in society. Influencing a shift of this magnitude is a staggering challenge, but it is one that we can meet with the right combination of market price signals and more coherent regulation. It is fundamentally not a change that can be forced or micromanaged by democratically elected governments. People will need to willingly adjust their behavior, and for that to occur, they will need to find value in the changes for themselves. This will require the market to innovate and adopt new lower-carbon solutions that create at least as much value as the high-carbon solutions in use today.

Although we are seeing positive developments in carbon-efficiency every day—improved building designs, lower-energy transportation solutions, virtual workplaces, Internet shopping, and the renewal of inner cities as desirable living spaces, to name a few—we're not there yet. The rapid and transformative change we need to meet emissions targets is not yet taking place. There is a real risk that despite our good intentions and steady progress, we will move too slowly to offset the effect of population and economic growth. Even when alternatives deliver equal value, people are slow to change patterns and behaviors.

And yet there is still hope. There *have* been historical examples of quick and dramatic shifts in human behavior over periods of time as short as a few decades. The personal computer went from initial introduction in the early 1980s to playing a central role in almost every aspect of business and our personal lives in a period of only twenty-five years. The cell phone and its associated network have completely changed the way people think about personal communications, and this is not just a developed-world phenomenon. About twenty years after the introduction of the first generally usable cell phones in 1991 at about the size and weight of a brick (an early 1990s version is pictured in figure 10.1), the cell phone has evolved into a versatile, Star Trek–like mobile personal communication device that has become ubiquitous, even in the developing world.[2] Mobile voice and text communication has leapfrogged landline technology and changed the way people everywhere work and conduct their lives.

What is this force that can cause people to change so quickly? It is, quite simply, *delight*. Delight is the holy grail of product developers. People experience delight when something surpasses their expectation. Beauty can delight, but so can efficiency. Delight brings people back again and again. Delight gets people over their aversion to change, so that change becomes the only meaningful path forward. This chapter looks at how delight can radically transform markets, and how we can lay the groundwork for innovations that are both carbon efficient *and* profoundly delightful.

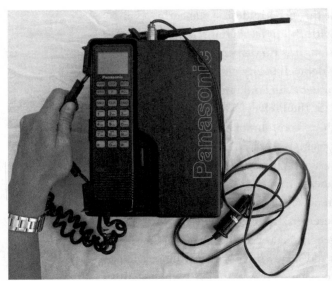

10.1. Evolution of cell phones from the early 1990s to 2011. Photos by A-P Hurd and Skene Howie

RECOGNIZING DELIGHT

Entering the Cluny–La Sorbonne station of the Paris metro, one finds the long arch of the ceiling over the rail track covered in mosaics depicting the signatures of all the great authors who have lived in the city: Moliere, Balzac, Simone de Beauvoir. All of those familiar signatures are writ large in blue on a white tile background. The scene is so unexpected it takes one's breath away. It transforms the experience of waiting for the train from an annoyance to be borne to a moment to be treasured. One is *sorry* when the train pulls into the station, blocking the view and putting an end to the experience. In fact, much of the Paris Metro system, from the art-nouveau entrances that invite travelers underground to the architecture of individual stations, is designed to inspire delight. It is one of the most well-loved and well-used transit systems in the world. It elicits not just satisfaction but passion. Now that's quite something for a transit system.

In Stockholm, Volkswagen engineers recently transformed the stairs leading out of the Odenplan metro station into a giant functioning piano keyboard, complete with sound. Many commuters immediately switched to this intriguing stairway to enjoy making musical sounds instead of using the adjacent escalator. Volkswagen reports that 66 percent more people are now using the stairway. Their spokesman commented: "Fun can obviously change behavior for the better."[3]

The tripling of the number of farmers' markets in the United States, from about seventeen hundred in 1994 to more than fifty-two hundred today (there are one hundred farmers' markets in New York City alone!) would not have happened if the phenomenon were simply a product of shoppers' nostalgia for a more rustic past.[4] What is it, then, that is bringing more people to these markets week after week? It seems highly unlikely that it is convenience, or variety, or economics—it is very hard to beat our abundant and efficient supermarkets on those counts. In our view, otherwise busy people are deciding to make that extra weekly shopping trip to the farmers' market simply because they *enjoy* doing it. Choosing fruit and vegetables that weren't bred primarily to be tough enough to travel for days in a truck and that taste so fresh that you can tell they were picked that morning can be a joy. Any lack of perfection in shape or size only adds to our satisfaction. To top it off, it is impossible to duplicate the "feel" for the food we get when we receive it from the hand of the farmer who grew it. Our point is not that we can solve our CO_2 problems if everyone starts using farmers' markets but rather that people will choose to do things that might otherwise seem inconvenient if they find delight in them.

Enrique Peñalosa—the former mayor of Bogotá, Colombia, who has achieved international renown for his accomplishments in urban design, transportation, and social programming—often speaks about the need to make public transportation "sexy." People won't ride it if it's not sexy, he says. Peñalosa speaks of the need to delight passengers with the quality, safety, and cleanliness of vehicles and with the speed and reliability of schedules. Only with these things in place can people be delighted enough to spur the massive transit adoption that can completely transform a region's access paradigm. The more people who adopt, the more service can be economically provided. The greater the range and frequency of service, the more it becomes a viable access and mobility network.

Peñalosa put his money where his mouth is. To inspire delight, the city purchased beautiful buses that look like rail cars and run on tires on the road. Bogotá built loading zones so that people could pay to enter the zone before the bus arrived and load/unload quickly and efficiently while the bus was at the platform. How did a city in Colombia accomplish this? Peñalosa and his administration bet so much on the system's potential to delight its customers that they rededicated existing lanes of highways exclusively to the buses, thereby avoiding the costs (and carbon impacts) of building new infrastructure. It worked. The traffic in the remaining lanes is no worse than it was before, bus rapid transit has become exceedingly time-competitive with automobile travel (in the case of many trips, it is substantially faster), and it has been widely adopted.[5] People are delighted with the choice they have been given, and Bogotá's citizens are proud of their transit system.

The critical question is how we can achieve a series of delight-inspiring innovations that will get us to a carbon-efficient economy quickly. A look at the rapid rise of the Internet and the World Wide Web is encouraging in this regard. In the mid-1960s two loosely related problems combined to create overlapping new network requirements. Military planners were concerned that their existing hierarchical data communication networks were completely dependent on a small number of central hubs and thus were highly vulnerable in a nuclear attack; they dreamed of a network that could survive the loss of significant components and still function. At the same time, researchers in universities were frustrated that their existing point-to-point networks did not facilitate the sharing of the information that had begun accumulating on their relatively new and powerful research computers. People working on both problems hypothesized that a nonhierarchical data network would provide a much more versatile and survivable medium for information exchange.

The researchers led the way in 1968, when the U.S. Advanced Research Project Agency (ARPA) issued a call to 140 potential bidders to quote on designing and building a prototype of such a network. Most computer science companies regarded the ARPA request as outlandish—only twelve submitted bids. But by December of 1969 the winning contractor, BBN Technologies, had successfully connected research facilities at UCLA, Stanford, the University of Utah, and the University of California–Santa Barbara, all using different commercial computers of the day. ARPANET was born.[6]

Over the next three decades, one development led rapidly to another. The number of ARPANET nodes grew by leaps and bounds almost immediately. Enhancements began springing up from a wide variety of sources, many of which were not government-funded. In the first fifteen years of ARPANET's existence, shared e-mail, file transfer, and a very robust communications backbone protocol all emerged, creating hitherto unimaginable flexibility for research information sharing. Driven by the economics of the growing user base, by the mid-1980s the network bandwidth had evolved from being largely government-funded to the current industry-funded model. By 1991, ARPANET had been transformed into the World Wide Web through advances in information indexing, improvements in the user interface, and the development of the system of embedding links in text to other text (called hypertext).

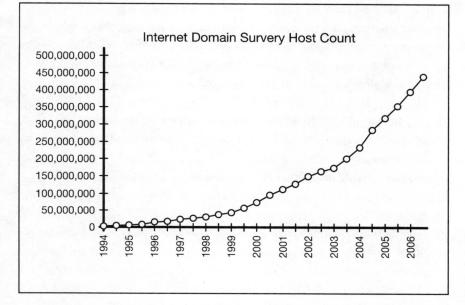

10.2. Internet domain (site) growth from 1994 to 2006. Source: Internet Software Consortium

The introduction in the early 1990s of graphical browsers and broadly available standard e-mail, the incorporation of Microsoft's Internet Explorer as an integral part of Windows 98, and the emergence of powerful search engines like Google made the Internet easily usable to everyone who had access to a PC.[7] People of all ages, not just trained computer specialists but members of the broad public, were surprised, delighted, and completely hooked by these new tools for communicating and finding information. As a result, throughout the 1990s the number of Internet users doubled every year, and by the year 2000 globally there were more than 360 million users.[8] The number of sites had grown to sixty million by that year.[9] Since then, the Internet has continued to evolve in many new directions, particularly with the advent of wireless technology and "edge" devices of all descriptions, to the point that it permeates almost everything we do. It is now used by an estimated 25 percent of the world's population (two billion people globally) because it provides such clear and delightful benefits.[10]

The climate change problem of the twenty-first century certainly differs substantially from the issues researchers were experiencing interconnecting their new computers in 1965. But the evolution of the Internet provides important lessons on how an open environment that provides a platform for innovation can be amazingly successful in fostering rapid, profound change.

In addition to the Internet, the personal computer, the cell phone, and the car, there are many other examples of rapidly accepted, world-changing innovations: universally available electric power, the telephone, the radio, and the airplane are but a few more. All of these developments occurred in environments that shared a number of common attributes:

» Key inventions played an important role, but the solutions were developed and brought into general use through the efforts of many innovators building on each other's work.

» The underlying ideas got off the ground in the private or research sectors, but government played a supporting role in fostering their development.

» They rapidly became available and affordable to a significant percentage of the population.

» They matured quickly in the near absence of regulation, in most cases because they were too new for existing regulations to apply to them.

» Most important, these key inventions improved the quality of life for the multitude; they created widespread delight.

Ultimately, these examples show that it takes a convergence of factors—from good ideas to a compelling business opportunity and a supportive regulatory environment—to catalyze the development and adoption of game-changing innovation.

HOW WE DELIGHT

STRATEGY #10: Set the stage for innovation. Don't constrain solutions; be prepared to face the glorious complexity of the problem and to be surprised by both elegant and patchwork solutions that emerge. Take risks and be confident that the breakthroughs we need will be the ones that inspire profound and widespread delight.

Governments

Encourage the development and flow of information, the critical enabler of change.

In her book *Leadership and the New Science*, the author and management consultant Margaret Wheatley refers to *information* as "the creative energy of the universe."[11] When writing about how systems change, she states: "Whenever the environment offers new and different information, the system chooses whether to accept the provocation and respond. . . . if the system pays attention to this information, it brings the information inside, and once inside that network, the information grows and changes. If the information becomes such a large disturbance that the system can no longer ignore it, then real change is at hand."[12]

Beginning in the late 1850s, the French chemist and microbiologist Louis Pasteur conducted a series of experiments demonstrating that fermentation was caused by the growth of microorganisms. His intuition that many diseases were also caused by similar microorganisms (rather than being "spontaneously generated") led to his confirmation of the germ theory of disease in 1878.[13] This development arguably puts Pasteur at "the top of the list of greatest benefactors of humanity" and illustrates how dramatically information can change the world.[14] Prior to Pasteur's popularization of the germ theory, people generally had little idea of what caused most diseases and unknowingly engaged in any number of unsanitary, life-threatening behaviors. Doctors routinely didn't bother washing their hands before performing surgery. The average lifespan in 1870 was forty-five years, primarily because parents often lost their children to what we would now consider to be very treatable illnesses (three of Pasteur's five children didn't survive to adulthood).

Then Pasteur made his findings known and, to use Wheatley's words, the system paid attention and real change was at hand. An ensuing period of discovery after discovery dramatically strengthened humans' hand in the battle with germs—pasteurization, immunization, sterilization of medical instruments, penicillin, and antibiotics. Basic sanitation was taught to adults and even to school children, and they adopted it wholeheartedly because it provided such obvious benefits to them. Since about 1870, after millennia of human life expectancy being stuck in the thirty- to forty-year range, public health has enjoyed a century of improvement that is nothing short of miraculous.[15] And the trigger for all this change was the information made available by Pasteur and his contemporaries.

Information can play two key roles in solving the carbon problem. First, and most obviously, we need knowledge about improved approaches to flow throughout the economy so that innovation can snowball, much as it did in the evolution of the Internet and health care. Second, and just as important, information about the causes and effects of climate change must be freely available, even in its glorious ambiguity. A significant portion of the population has at least a latent concern about the risks of greenhouse gases. Most people would like to know "the facts" but are confused by all of the noise surrounding climate change. A continued flow of more refined information is critical to helping them understand the situation.

Wheatley has argued that the disorder caused by new information is necessary to awaken the creativity that can be the source of a new order that is often more robust than the old order.[16] Governments were on the right track in 1989 when they established the Intergovernmental Panel on Climate Change (IPCC) in response to concerns about the information available on climate change, notwithstanding the 2009 controversy over leaked documents from the agency.[17] Despite the fact that climate change skeptics made much of some of the leaked material, the very public discourse at that time led to numerous serious media reports on the science of climate change. This is good because we need all of the information we can get on the complex question of climate change to be in the public domain. The better the public understands the situation, the more likely people are to be delighted by elegant solutions to the carbon problem. Governments therefore must treat the continued development of reliable information on climate change as an important public good and foster the refinement of it by continuing to support such bodies as the IPCC as well as other research on the subject.

Find politically acceptable ways to foster carbon-reducing innovation.

Throughout this book we have explored the strategies required to facilitate a carbon-efficient economy. We have talked about how governments can help exploit technologies that already exist. But perhaps the greatest challenge for governments is to open the door to new and delightful things that haven't yet been imagined. A great deal more ingenuity is needed to create the level of delight that will lead to widespread adoption. It is critically important for governments to recognize that we have not yet seen the kind of innovation and market change that will lead to climate stability. Unfortunately, unlike the Internet or many other examples of technological innovation, the built environment is anything but a new field of endeavor. Establishing a fertile environment for creativity goes against the grain of many of the painstakingly crafted regulations and frameworks that govern buildings, development, and land use.

In most of the dramatic change scenarios cited earlier in this chapter, governments could more or less stand by and wait to see what the market produced. In the case of the built environment, our regulatory legacy makes it imperative that governments play an active role in setting the stage for carbon-efficient innovation. Policy makers must aggressively identify and eliminate historical barriers and seek new approaches that will allow the private sector to test and implement new solutions. Certainly governments are congenitally poor at taking risks. However, there are a number of steps they can take to support carbon-reducing change. With the right frameworks in place, governments can foster innovation, even in such a tradition-bound domain as the built environment. In particular governments must:

» Allow the private sector increased leeway for innovation with respect to existing regulations—for instance, through clearly identified pilot projects that can shorten approval cycles and reduce the political fallout from not-so-successful experiments.

» Create industry panels and boards (separate from traditional staff and agency review processes) to review and manage risk on particularly groundbreaking or disruptive applications of new technologies.

» Work energetically with the private sector to identify and remove barriers in existing regulation.

» Where possible, provide financial incentives or assistance to specific proof-of-concept projects.

» Avoid tying up public funds and other resources in long-term subsidies of new solutions; approaches that have a real future will need to stand on their own feet, and any public funding that can be made available is better spent on supporting new innovation.

» Engage in an ongoing public communication campaign aimed at helping the public and the media understand that the goal is to foster much more innovation (with some inevitable setbacks) because it is really needed.

In British Columbia a development consortium in Victoria has completed the initial phase of the first complete neighborhood to target LEED Platinum certification for buildings developed in a master-planned community. Although completion of the full project has been slowed by the 2008 recession, the planned fifteen-acre mixed-use development, called Dockside Green (being built on a reclaimed industrial site near the harbor), is garnering international attention. The design incorporates three compact neighborhoods with plenty of green spaces, a network of walking and bicycle paths, good access to public transportation, and flowing naturalized creeks fed by storm and fully treated wastewater. The focus on sustainability is evident everywhere in the development, including in the green roofs, the choice of building materials, and the low-energy heating and cooling systems.

The City of Victoria does not bill residents for the sewage component of the normal local water bill because the project includes on-site treatment of 100 percent of wastewater (which includes heat and gas recovery). The 1.3-million-square-foot development inspires genuine pride, even delight, in its residents and members of the public. The city has been very transparent about the experimental nature of the project, indicating that it is closely following the impact this kind of development will have on both Victoria and the surrounding region. It has established a public monitoring process, requiring Dockside Green to submit annual sustainability reports that are posted on the city's Web site.[18] Dockside Green is a living demonstration of how developers and government can cooperate to sustain broad public support for a project that challenges existing norms through good design, a clear focus on the environment, and enlightened public communication.

Environmental Nonprofits

Support innovation responsibly.

....

In the campaign for carbon reduction, environmental nonprofits must not lose sight of three key points:

» The number-one priority is to foster the necessary innovation to achieve significant carbon reduction, and there is a long way to go on this front.
» Innovation involves trial and error and therefore risk; mistakes and wrong directions are inevitable and need to be kept in perspective.
» The magnitude of the challenge and the urgency of the situation will require an unprecedented level of collaboration between governments and the development industry.

Because they are not aligned with either governments or developers, environmental nonprofits have a critical role to play. They can choose to foster (or not to foster) a discourse and media environment that encourages risk-taking. They can applaud politicians who work on creating room to breathe in a tightly controlled regulatory environment, or they can bring them down at the least misstep. In the inevitable controversy that will surround public experiments in carbon reduction, the media will often turn to environmental nonprofits for knowledgeable third-party opinion. These organizations can make an important positive contribution to the debate if they recognize that progress toward their goals cannot be achieved without trial and error. They have a critical role to play in creating the safe space to fail for both governments and private enterprise. Without their understanding and acceptance of failures—an integral part of the innovative process—we can never achieve the kind of transformative and delightful innovation we so desperately need.

In some cases this responsibility may require environmental nonprofits to examine and possibly adjust or broaden the interests on which they were founded. In chapter 7 we talked about how Forterra evolved from a focus on rural spaces to believing that the organization could best protect natural spaces by supporting denser development within the urban growth boundary. Environmental nonprofits, whether or not it is their primary mandate, have tremendous potential to facilitate or impede progress on carbon reduction in the built environment. It is our hope that when called upon, they will subject their advocacy to a reasonableness test against the three factors listed earlier in this section.

Investors and Developers

Try new ways to make money from carbon and energy efficiency.

....

In this book's introduction, we mentioned the hurdles developers face in attempting to achieve carbon reduction in the built environment. In the subsequent chapters, we have tried to clear the path by advising other institutions on the steps they must to take to make lower-carbon development viable. But even if these other players heed all of the advice we have offered, the heavy lifting of developing, testing, and implementing delightful carbon-reducing solutions will fall to investors and developers. No progress is possible without the private sector being willing to do things differently than before. Although the risk-return equation underlies all investment decisions, private sector participants need to be willing entrepreneurs in exploring the possibilities for making money on this new playing field. If they keep doing business as usual, they will have squandered the opportunity that has been painstakingly given to them. Just as other institutions need to shed some of their tradition-bound ways of doing things, so do for-profit businesses. This is not as automatic as one might think. There are countless stories of industrial giants whose downfall has been brought about by their determined focus on the old way of doing things in the face of the potential for transformative change. Just ask the folks who used be part of the Underwood Typewriter Company.

Consider the economic potential of entrepreneurs who took the opposite tack: Henry Ford did not invent the car, but he understood its potential, and his vision and determination made it available to the masses and brought enormous success to his enterprise. Investors and developers will need to make a similar entrepreneurial effort to stay abreast of developments in this field, participating in carbon-reducing pilot projects and actively considering how to incorporate carbon-reducing technologies into their mainstream projects. Some examples of practices that immediately deserve more consideration include greater use of natural cooling, unbundling parking from commercial space leases, and offering individual energy metering for commercial tenants.

Perhaps even greater potential for investors and entrepreneurs lies in finding carbon-efficient combinations of the vast array of new technologies that have emerged over the past few decades. Consider wind farms and cloud computing. These two technologies might seem to have little in common, but there may be a synergy between them that has yet to be exploited. The biggest challenge in effectively harnessing wind energy is its inherent variability; demand for energy doesn't vary with the local wind speed. As a result, wind power has sometimes been paired with hydro- or thermal power, but this leads to duplication of generating capacity. The other solution—storing wind energy—has been limited by growth in battery capacity.

What if we could find a way to vary power demand as the wind waxes and wanes? The expansion of cloud computing over the next several years might present an opportunity. Cloud technology already allows information technology services to be provided from an array of computer "servers," and cloud technology moves the workload transparently and instantaneously among these computer servers to manage demand. It could be possible to pair wind farms with cloud server farms and let the cloud automatically migrate the computing load to the servers where there was power available. If you were downloading a movie to your home computer, for instance, the download would come from whatever servers had the wind blowing nearby. If the wind dropped, the download would just shift to another cloud computing/wind farm location. This might require greater redundancy in (relatively cheap) servers but could overcome the need to invest in redundant generation or storage capacity.

Even for those businesses that don't consider themselves early adopters, the economics can be compelling. Whether because of climate change or energy security policies, there is no question that the price of fossil fuel energy will rise in the coming decades. Even the American auto industry (not always known for being ahead of the curve) is betting on this trend with a bevy of lower-energy vehicles. Developers who ignore this trend put themselves at a competitive disadvantage. But those who hone their expertise in low-carbon techniques not only lower risk and future-proof their portfolios; they also contribute to mainstreaming the technological and financing innovations that are coming to market. Some developers are already learning to build and renovate low-carbon buildings with capital and operating cost structures that are competitive with older techniques; these buildings are likely to command a premium price in the future because of better long-term value and because of their ability to delight the public.

Work closely with government to establish an effective environment for carbon-reducing innovation.

Many developers' interaction with government is focused at a local level on entitling individual projects. Within this framework there is often mistrust and little opportunity to shift the paradigm in which the parties are working together. In countless jurisdictions across the country, developers bemoan the narrow mindedness of planners and review boards; meanwhile the planners and review boards cast skeptical eyes at the motivations of the money-grubbing developers. Not really the ideal scenario for policy collaboration.

Nonetheless, there is a critical need for both parties to get together outside the instance of a specific project and find common ground for policy solutions. Lawmakers, policy makers, and planners need to be willing to listen. Conversely, developers need to play an active role in finding solutions. They cannot expect policy makers to be mind readers, intuitively understanding what the private sector needs. Developers need to find allies in the research and nonprofit sectors who can validate their approach and give environmental policy makers the air cover to work closely with the private sector. Developers need to do the work to articulate good solutions that meet climate change goals *and* allow them to do business profitably. They cannot just say "no" in the face of the oncoming train, and they need to give feedback to continue tweaking the changes that do take place. Nearly all policy decisions have unintended consequences, and developers will need to come back to the table, even after the first round, to keep making things work better.

DELIGHT IN A NUTSHELL

For carbon-efficient products and services to achieve widespread adoption, stakeholders at all levels need to strive for solutions that delight consumers. Delight-inspiring solutions are usually the product of free-flowing information and innovation. The private sector is in the best position to manage the risk associated with innovating, but governments and nonprofits have a role to play in facilitating innovation. We should not lose sight of two key facts: we still have some distance to go, and we are all new at this.

CHAPTER 11

MAKING A DENT

Unless someone like you cares a whole awful lot, nothing is going to get better. It's not.

—DR. SEUSS

Throughout this book we have described the strategies that can consequentially impact carbon emissions from the built environment. Even more important, we've set out to articulate some specific tools and levers that each of our institutions has at its disposal, and which tools are most appropriate to make the shift to a carbon-efficient economy. Some of the examples may become dated as our buildings and land use patterns continue to evolve, but the fundamental ideas behind measuring the right thing, sending clear price signals, and inspiring delight can continue to inform our efforts for years to come. If you've powered through the book, you're probably unusual. In a world with so much information, the most common strategy to deal with complexity is to look for a summary or to focus on a few narrow areas. But if your interest lies in trying to understand how to make all the pieces come together, not only are you unusual but you are well placed to make a difference in finding the solution. The challenge of climate change at this point may well present the most compelling need and opportunity we have ever faced to rethink a broad range of systems, rules, and incentives. But if we are to successfully reorganize so many of our existing economic systems and institutions to reduce our carbon footprint, we desperately need generalists.

Much of the early thinking on how to reduce carbon intensity has been done by visionaries. Their work has been critical to understanding some of the most essential elements of what we need to change and where we need to head. But visionaries and altruists will never make up enough critical mass to solve the problem. There will never be enough virtuous vegetarians to make a real difference (even if their carbon footprints are one car lower per capita than the average American meat eater). Even if 20 percent of the population moved right off the grid, we wouldn't begin to make the dent we need. To reverse our upward trajectory in energy use (and CO_2 production) and to reach emissions targets that are well below today's levels, while maintaining economic growth and quality of life, we need everyone—even the people who don't care—to change quite a lot of what they are doing.

This book is about maintaining choices while giving consumers financial transparency into their impact on the planet. It's about monetizing "virtuous" behavior into something tangible that can be considered in every purchasing decision. We believe it is possible to consequentially change how much CO_2 the average American produces while maintaining the essential American values of freedom and capitalism. This book addresses how coordinated and systemic policy frameworks can improve the lives of all our citizens while they generate less and less carbon dioxide. We can only achieve this goal with an integrative approach at every level, combined with an ability to see the history, the big picture, the motivations and needs of the participants in our economies and our communities. If we don't work across the system, interacting with the efforts of others and with a fundamental awareness of economic forces, we will not achieve the magnitude of change we desperately need to create an insurance policy for the future.

It is our hope that we have provided a roadmap that will allow readers to be in the vanguard of the next generation of carbon-change agents. Citizens throughout this country's civic, political, or economic life have the opportunity to bring a systems view, to make connections, to do the hard work of revisiting old rules, old policies, and old ways of doing things and ask the brave question—sometimes again and again: Is this *truly* economically efficient and carbon-efficient? We have the opportunity to think hard about what our utilities, our gas gauges, and our wallets really measure. We can demand that policies and budgets be administered at an appropriate level of jurisdiction that creates the most public value for our tax dollars. We have a right to question existing frameworks and to strive for outcome-based measures that will foster innovation. We have an obligation to move these questions into the public discourse about the solution to climate change.

If we set our minds to it, we have the knowledge and the ability to achieve a carbon-efficient economy. We just need to get out there and make a dent.

Notes

INTRODUCTION

1. Boden, Marland, and Andres, *Global, Regional, and National Fossil-Fuel CO_2 Emissions.*

2. Taylor and Standing, "Drought in Australia Food Bowl Continues."

3. Eckert, "World 2009 CO_2 Emissions Off by 1.3%."

4. Meadows, *Thinking in Systems*, 145–65.

5. United Nations Environmental Programme (UNEP), Maps and Graphics tab, "World Greenhouse Gas Emissions by Sector," data for 2000, online at http://maps .grida.no/go/graphic/world-greenhouse-gas-emissions-by-sector (accessed May 30, 2011). Our calculation that the built environment accounts for 77 percent of carbon emissions is based on this data.

6. Alexander, Ishikawa, and Silverstein, *Pattern Language.*

7. This book uses the term *institutions* to refer to individuals or enterprises that are part of our society and our economy, and who interact with others while pursuing their own goals. In outlining our ten key strategies related to reducing carbon emissions from the built environment, we discuss different levels of agency, which include the federal government, state governments, local governments, environmental nonprofits, private sector companies, developers, investors, educational institutions, and individuals. Clearly, there are other actors and institutions in our society, but these were the ones with the most differentiation in their ability to impact emissions. That being said, it is useful to define the scope of a few of the terms we use to describe agency.

    Environmental nonprofits refers to not-for-profit organizations whose primary or corollary mission is to protect our environment. Not all environmental nonprofits are focused on the challenge in the same way. Some, like the Environmental Working Group, work in public education and advocacy for policy. Others, like the National Center for Safe Routes to School, build community- and neighborhood-based programs. Others, like the U.S. Green Building Council, serve as clearinghouses for best environmental practices in a particular industry. Still others, like the Rocky Mountain Institute, engage in primary research that contributes to our understanding of climate change and potential solutions. Recognizing these differences, not all recommendations will apply to all environmental nonprofits. However, if they wish to transform the thinking and practice around climate change, they must—in aggregate—foster and even create many pieces of the solution.

Private sector companies and developers refer to profit-driven companies of all sizes that are publicly or privately held. These enterprises generate much of the productivity, wealth, and true job growth in our society. We assume that these companies need to remain profitable and that they will not compromise profitability to meet some other altruistic goal, however appealing it may be. *Real estate developers* are technically a subset of private sector companies, but they are occasionally separated out for the purposes of detailing a specific strategy because they have a particular vantage point from which they can influence decisions about land use and the built environment. In a sense, developers are the lens of risk management through which innovations in the built environment are vetted and products and processes are adopted.

Investors refers to a specific subset of private sector companies. Sometimes we discuss investors separately for two reasons: First, investment strategies, even by large groups, represent the aggregated perceptions of many individuals. As such, many investments are group decisions based on a shared analysis methodology. The methodologies in use at any time influence the kind of investments that are viable. In 2010 few people invested in Catholic cathedrals or commercial mortgage-backed securities loans, but both of these investments have seemed appropriate under past investment strategies. Second, the investor category in this book refers to the more "passive" player in the money-execution partnership. The investor may provide guidelines but often does not make day-to-day management decisions. Therefore, an investor's influence on CO_2 emissions is in a different sphere than that of the company executive or the real estate developer.

Governments refers to the federal, state, and local levels of government. The recipe for successful government participation in CO_2 reduction begins with actions at an appropriate level of agency. In the United States different levels of government are responsible for different aspects of the public good mandate. For example, state governments are the primary administrators of education. The federal government manages the interstate road network. Given the policy scope of each level of government, there are clearly different levels of intervention that are most appropriate for federal, state, and local governments. Identifying the appropriate level of agency on climate change for different levels of government is a key goal of this book.

8.   Stern, *Global Deal*.

1 / MEASURE FOR MEASURE

1. CME Group, a CME/Chicago Board of Trade /NYMEX Company, available online at http://www.cmegroup.com/trading/commodities/livestock/frozen-pork-bellies_contract_specifications.html (accessed May 30, 2011). Specifications for pork belly contracts were obtained at this site.

2. Ball, "Six Products, Six Carbon Footprints."

3. Ibid.

4. Wikipedia, s.v. "PDCA," last updated May 26, 2011, online at http://en.wikipedia .org/wiki/PDCA (accessed May 30, 2011).

5. International Organization for Standardization, "Discover ISO: The Scope of ISO's Work," online at http://www.iso.org/iso/about/discover-iso_the-scope-of-isos-work .htm (accessed June 22, 2011).

6. See Center for Neighborhood Technology (CNT), "H+T Affordability Index," online at http://www.htaindex.org/method.php (accessed May 30, 2011).

7. CNT, "HUD and DOT Secretaries Declare Groundbreaking Partnership to Link Housing and Transportation Policy," online at http://www.cnt.org/news/ 2009/03/20/hud-and-dot-secretaries-declare-groundbreaking-partnership-to-link-housing-and-transportation-policy (accessed May 20, 2011).

2 / THE INVISIBLE HAND

1. "Big Mac Index," *Economist.com,* online at http://www.economist.com/node/ 21524873 (accessed August 29, 2011).

2. Smith, *Inquiry into the Nature and Causes.*

3. Mikael Riknäs, "Universal Chargers to Finally Become a Reality," *PC World,* February 17, 2009. Riknäs indicates that a standard for the mobile phone power connection plug may finally emerge in the next few years; online at http://www.pcworld.com/ article/159630/universal_chargers_to_finally_become_a_reality.html (accessed May 30, 2011).

4. Wikipedia, s.v. "Videotape format war," last updated June 2, 2011, online at http://en.wikipedia.org/wiki/Videotape_format_war (accessed June 25, 2011).

5. "Plane Truths," *The Economist.*

6. Although all the references we discovered attributed this quotation to Buckminster Fuller, we could not locate a proven source for it. The Buckminster Fuller Institute advised us that they have been asked about the quotation many times. They believe it to have originated from Buckminster Fuller, but they have been unable to locate an actual, documentable source for it. This is apparently not unusual with respect to quotations attributed to Buckminster Fuller, in part because of the extensiveness of his writings and his very frequent and lengthy lectures.

7. U.S. Conference of Mayors, "Mayors Leading the Way on Climate Protection," online at http://www.usmayors.org/climateprotection/revised/ (accessed June 25, 2011).

8. For details on the Acid Rain Program, see U.S. Environmental Protection Agency, "Cap and Trade." U.S. Environmental Protection Agency Newsroom, "Power Plants Continue to Decrease SO2 Emissions under EPA Cap and Trade Program," December 11, 2009, online at http://yosemite.epa.gov/opa/admpress.nsf/6427a6b753895 5c585257359003f0230/bdf208410089b5c185257689005e2577!OpenDocument (accessed June 25, 2011).

9. U.S. Department of Transportation, Research and Innovative Technology Administration (RITA), Bureau of Transportation Statistics, "Table 1–11: Number of U.S. Aircraft, Vehicles, Vessels, and Other Conveyances," online at http://www.bts.gov/publications/national_transportation_statistics/html/table_01_11.html (accessed June 27, 2011). The table indicates that there were 255,917,664 registered vehicles in the United States in 2008. Also see U.S. Census Bureau, "American Housing Survey (AHS)," FAQs, online at http://www.census.gov/hhes/www/housing/ahs/ahsfaq.html (accessed June 25, 2011).

10. British Columbia Ministry of Finance, "Tax Cuts Funded by Carbon Tax," online at http://www.fin.gov.bc.ca/tbs/tp/climate/A2.htm (accessed June 25, 2011).

11. Allers and Hoeben, "Effects of Unit-Based Garbage Pricing," 426. A study in the Netherlands found that user fees in that country reduced garbage quantities by averages of 24 percent for unsorted waste and by 46 percent for biodegradable waste. Reductions were even higher if the fee was weight-based rather than bin-based.

12. Service Canada, "GST/HST Credit," online at http://www.servicecanada.gc.ca/eng/goc/gst_credit.shtml (accessed June 25, 2011).

13. U.S. Energy Information Administration, "Annual Energy Review 2009," Figure 8.2a, "Electricity Net Generation Total (All Sectors)," online at http://www.eia.doe.gov/emeu/aer/elect.html (accessed June 25, 2011).

14. U.S. Energy Information Administration (EIA). "Form EIA-860, 'Annual Electric Generator Report,' - Generator (Existing) File," with the subheading "This file represents existing generators as of December 31, 2008." The figure of two thousand natural gas and coal-generating plants in the United States was obtained from this Excel file provided by the EIA, online at http://www.eia.doe.gov/cneaf/electricity/page/capacity/existingunitsbs2008.xls (accessed June 25, 2011).

15. Nader and Heaps, "We Need a Global Carbon Tax." This opinion piece in the *Wall Street Journal* makes the case for why the important economies in the world might be inclined to cooperate on the implementation of a global carbon tax.

3 / REGULATORY ROADBLOCKS

1. "Recycling and Reusable Cups," *Starbucks Global Responsibility Report: Goals and Progress 2010*, online at http://www.starbucks.com/responsibility/learn-more/goals-and-progress/recycling#open (accessed June 14, 2011).

2. Ibid.

3. Ewing et al., *Growing Cooler,* 132–33.

4. Sharman, "Why Wind Power Works in Denmark," 66.

5. Wikipedia, s.v. "Net Metering," last updated June 2, 2011, online at http://en
.wikipedia.org/wiki/Net_metering (accessed June 25, 2011).

6. Wikipedia, s.v. "Electric power transmission," last updated August 28, 2011, online
at http://en.wikipedia.org/wiki/Electric_power_transmission (accessed August 30,
2011). Power losses in transmission in the United States in 2007 were estimated to be
6.5 percent of power produced. Also see Natural Resources Defense Council, "The
Future Role of Nuclear Power in the United States," online at http://www.nrdc.org/
nuclear/pnucpwr.asp (accessed June 25, 2011).

7. Lund et al., "Danish Wind Power Export and Cost," 21.

8. Ibid., 29.

9. Arizona Power Authority, "Hoover Dam," online at http://www.powerauthority.org/
index.php?name=Sections&req=viewarticle&artid=5&page=1 (accessed June 25,
2011).

10. ITE, *Trip Generation.*

4 / REDUCE

1. NAHB, *Housing Facts,* 14.

2. Diamond and Moezzi, *Changing Trends,* figure 2; the figure is based on 2003 Energy
Information Administration data. It shows that U.S. annual per capita residential
energy use (from electricity, gas, coal, oil, and wood) over the thirty-year period from
1970 to 2000 has been essentially flat at about 70 Mbtu. From 1950 to 1970 annual
per capital energy consumption rose steadily from 40 Mbtu to 70 Mbtu. NABH,
Housing Facts, 44. In 1970, 34 percent of new homes in the United States had
central air-conditioning installed versus 90 percent in 2004. Also see U.S. Energy
Information Administration, "Share of Energy"; appliances and electronics share of
household energy consumption rose from 17 percent to 31 percent in the twenty-
seven years between 1978 and 2005.

3. Phillips, "Builders Downsize the Dream Home," A1.

4. Darlin, "Street Corners vs. Cul de Sacs." Leinberger, "Next Slum?" 3.

5. Public Policy Institute of California, *PPIC Statewide Survey,* 10.

6. Ibid.

7. E-mail exchange between Julia Levitt (University of Washington graduate student)
and Tumbleweed Tiny House Company, January 10, 2010.

8. Lyttle, "Think Small," 1. Also see "Answers," B4Ubuild.com, online at
http://www.b4ubuild.com/faq/faq_0002.shtml (accessed June 25, 2011).

9. Wikipedia, s.v. "Milk," last updated June 23, 2011, online at http://en.wikipedia.org/
wiki/Milk (accessed June 25, 2011).

10. Bernstein, "Testimony of Scott Bernstein," 18.

11. American Automobile Association (AAA), "Your Driving Costs, 2008
Edition," online at http://www.aaanewsroom.net/Assets/Files/200844921220
.DrivingCosts2008.pdf (accessed June 25, 2011). AAA calculates that in 2008 a
medium sedan driven fifteen thousand miles per year cost 55.2 cents per mile, or

$8,280 per year to operate. The same vehicle driven ten thousand miles per year cost $7,190 per year to operate. A small sedan driven ten thousand miles per year cost $6,315 per year.

12. Nicole Gotthelf, Center for Neighborhood Technology (CNT), director of Development and Communications, e-mail message to Julia Levitt, January 11, 2010.

13. Pryne, "Modern Rooming House."

14. U.S. Green Building Council, *LEED 2009 for Existing Buildings: Operations & Maintenance,* online at http://www.usgbc.org/DisplayPage.aspx?CMSPageID=221 (accessed June 26, 2011).

15. Australian Government, Department of Climate Change and Energy Efficiency, "Buildings," online at http://www.environment.gov.au/sustainability/ energyefficiency/buildings/ (accessed June 22, 2011).

16. Legislative Assembly of Ontario, "Bill 101, Home Energy Rating Act, 2008," online at http://www.ontla.on.ca/web/bills/bills_detail.do?locale=en&BillID=2059 (accessed June 26, 2011). The proposed legislation would require that the seller of any residential building provide a home energy rating report to the prospective buyer in a defined format.

17. Jones Lang LaSalle, "Third Annual Sustainability Survey Finds Companies Are Considering Green Building and Energy Ratings in Making Leasing Decisions," online at http://www.joneslanglasalle.com.au/Australia/en-AU/Pages/NewsItem .aspx?ItemID=18260 (accessed June 26, 2011). A survey conducted in Australia in 2009 found that "70 percent of respondents considered sustainability to be a critical business issue and 89 percent considered sustainability criteria in their location decisions," up from 69 and 81 percent, respectively, in 2008.

18. LessEn, "Mobile App—See the Energy Rating of Workplaces around You," online at http://www.less-en.org/?page=MobileApp (accessed June 26, 2011).

19. Hybrid Cars, "Better Gas Mileage in a Toyota Prius," online at http://www .hybridcars.com/gas-saving-tips/maximizing-mileage-toyota-prius.html (accessed June 26, 2011).

20. Fuller, "Life Cycle Cost Analysis."

21. McNichols, "Rise and Fall of Air Conditioning." Weber Thompson, "New Logo Celebrates New Headquarters," press release, online at http://www.weberthompson .com/pressreleases/prterrythomas080415.html (accessed June 26, 2011).

22. Our estimate that the savings associated with avoiding the cost of air-conditioning is equivalent to the approximate cost of five days of employee time is based on the following model: The average fully loaded cost for a typical office worker is in the range of $70,000 per year or $266 per working day; the average space allocated per worker is two hundred square feet and the annual space cost with air-conditioning per worker is $30 per square foot or $6,000 per year; the annual space cost without air-conditioning is 75 percent of a/c space or $4,500 per worker, a savings of $1,500 per employee; and it would take 5.6 lost "too-hot-to-work" days at $266 per day to offset the $1,500 savings achieved by avoiding the cost of air-conditioning ($1,500 ÷ $266 ≃ 5.6). If the average fully loaded cost for a typical office worker is less than our mod-

elled $70,000 per year, it would take even more lost days before the breakeven point is reached. If the space allocation per worker is less than two hundred square feet, the breakeven point would be fewer days.

5 / BUILT TO LAST

1. Goodwill, "Donation FAQ's," http://www.horizongoodwill.org/donationfaq.html (accessed June 26, 2011).

2. The Distillery District, online at http://www.thedistillerydistrict.com/ (accessed June 26, 2011).

3. The Impact Investor, "Rose Smart Growth Investment Fund: Repairing and Greening the Fabric of Cities," online at http://www.theimpactinvestor.com/rose-smart-growth-investmen.html (accessed June 26, 2011).

4. Container City, online at http://www.containercity.com/ (accessed June 26, 2011).

5. Wikipedia, s.v. "Container City," last updated May 28, 2011, online at http://en.wikipedia.org/wiki/Container_City (accessed June 26, 2011).

6. Marohn, "Habitat ReStore Outlets Growing."

7. Greenfab News and Media, "The 99k House from Hybrid Seattle," June 9, 2009, online at http://www.greenfab-media.com/building-and-design/344/the-99k-house-from-hybrid-seattle (accessed June 26, 2011).

8. Michael Pyatok to Al Hurd, e-mail, July 5, 2011. In his e-mail Pyatok explains: "By high quality design I mean not only sensitive to the social and economic realities of the residents, and sensitive to conserving energy, materials and water, but also sensitive to their cultural origins and the cultural expectations of surrounding neighbors. All of these together make [a housing project] a landmark that everyone cherishes and wants to preserve generations later."

9. Wilson, Marcheski, and Hinckley, "Great PACE Controversy," 1–2. The Wilson paper contains a good description of how PACE financing was designed to work as well as a balanced discussion of the issues that the PACE financing scheme has encountered.

10. Federal Housing Finance Agency, "FHFA Statement on Certain Energy Retrofit Loan Programs," press release, July 6, 2010, online at http://www.fhfa.gov/webfiles/15884/PACESTMT7610.pdf (accessed June 24, 2011).

11. Wilson, Marcheski, and Hinckley, "Great PACE Controversy," 5.

12. Kate Knight, e-mail to A-P Hurd, June 24, 2011. The approach we advocate for resolving PACE issues collaboratively is based on Knight's recommendations.

13. Monterey Regional Waste Management District, "Last Chance Mercantile Quick Link," online at http://www.mrwmd.org/last-chance-mercantile.htm (accessed June 27, 2011).

14. Town of Los Altos Hills, "Your Guide to Deconstruction Permits," undated pamphlet published by Town of Los Altos Hills, California, Building Department, online at http://docs.google.com/viewer?a=v&q=cache:_T8TjLcTiNYJ:www.losaltoshills. ca.gov/doc-browse/doc_download/163-deconstruction-permit-brochure+Los+Altos+

Hills+your+guide+to+deconstruction+permits&hl=en&gl=ca&pid=bl&srcid=ADGE
ESjBedjfDBZKW_q_cxoyZnGoa1mzgubISwTv4Y-rKe3S1tCI2IYesrHhd7waI3Ud-
cph9RDohhB35aMS9ZNmIDu3dYWXFJCf0xSh-GukRie79nLe07S2abkJyW_3J_
JPqwk37Ah8R&sig=AHIEtbQjlYPQRFzLRizZDt-rqQfBZ7rMsQ (accessed June
27, 2011). Under the heading "Free Deconstruction Permits," this pamphlet explains
how to qualify under a November 2007 resolution passed by City Council "to waive
demolition permits fees for deconstruction of buildings for recycling purposes."

15. U.S. Green Building Council, "What LEED Is."

16. Little, *Power Trip,* 333.

6 / GREAT NEIGHBORHOODS

1. Rosenthal, "In German Suburb, Life Goes On."

2. Carsten Sperling, "Planning of the Vauban District Living and Mobility Concept,"
online at http://docs.google.com/viewer?a=v&q=cache:CIjjURbdnikJ:webcast
.ec.europa.eu/eutv/portal/pdfgenerator%3Fid%3D1466+planning+of+the+Vauban
+District+Living&hl=en&gl=ca&pid=bl&srcid=ADGEESgx1WCpJQkOttrQaz8TB
AQyaOOQ1_eAcQ6MMr3_vF-Wqpz_85j1_SVc2v3rByGYXkTXPeN9ZgrjgY0
MxPD9ZmUpOMTyMl8AWHb-NKQtOQG3nIxKB3dShUCPHeyghZAoNYS
aWZuh&sig=AHIEtbTezZLKXNr1MIVQDd15hje0JN4uGA (accessed June 28,
2011).

3. Frank Schäfer, architect in Freiburg, Germany, e-mail interview with Julia Levitt,
April 23, 2010.

4. City of Toronto, "College Street Avenues Study—Study Report (Trinity-
Spadina, Wards 19 and 20)," January 25, 2005, online at http://www.toronto.ca/
legdocs/2005/agendas/council/cc050412/te3rpt/cl004.pdf (accessed June 28, 2011).

5. Jeff Markowiak, Toronto city planning, e-mail to Julia Levitt, June 14, 2010.

6. American Automobile Association (AAA), "Your Driving Costs, 2008 Edition,"
online at http://www.aaanewsroom.net/Assets/Files/200844921220.DrivingCosts
2008.pdf (accessed June 25, 2011). AAA calculates that in 2008 a medium sedan
driven fifteen thousand miles a year cost 55.2 cents a mile, or $8,280 a year to oper-
ate. The same vehicle driven ten thousand miles a year cost $7,190 a year to operate.
A small sedan driven ten thousand miles a year cost $6,315 a year.

7. U.S. Department of Transportation Office of Public Affairs, "DOT Secretary Ray
LaHood."

8. Ewing et al., *Growing Cooler*; and Cambridge Systematics, *Moving Cooler.*

9. Front Seat, "Walk Score" link, online at http://www.frontseat.org/about.html
(accessed June 28, 2011).

10. Jacobs, *Death and Life of Great American Cities,* 40–44.

11. Seattle City Council, "Updating Seattle's Multifamily Code—Lowrise," online at
http://www.seattle.gov/council/clark/2009townhomes.htm (accessed June 28, 2011).

12. Robert Humble, e-mail interview with Julia Levitt, June 16, 2010.

13. Beatley and Newman, *Green Urbanism Down Under,* 25–27.

14. Australian Bureau of Statistics, "2006 Census QuickStats: Subiaco (State Suburb)," last updated October 25, 2007, online at http://www.censusdata.abs.gov.au/ABSNavigation/prenav/LocationSearch?collection=Census&period=2006&areacode=SSC52361&producttype=QuickStats&breadcrumb=PL&action=401 (accessed September 13, 2011).

7 / SPACES FOR NATURE

1. Bill Reed, in conversation with A-P Hurd and confirmed in an e-mail, May 19, 2010.
2. Biomimicry Institute, "Transportation: Learning Efficiency from Kingfishers," available online at http://www.biomimicryinstitute.org/case-studies/case-studies/transportation.html (accessed June 28, 2011).
3. Benyus, "What Do You Mean by Biomimicry?" Benyus provides a detailed explanation of biomimicry on this Web page of the Biomimicry Institute. She includes a summary of more than a dozen practical examples of work going on in the biometric field, including such things as studying how a leaf captures energy in hopes of creating a molecular-sized solar cell and mimicking the spider's process to find a way of manufacturing fibers without heat.
4. Nowak and Crane, "Carbon Storage and Sequestration," Section 3.2, 385.
5. Ibid., Section 3.4, 387.
6. Carver, Unger, and Parks, "Modeling Energy Savings."
7. Bruner Foundation Inc., "2009 Rudy Bruner Award: Silver Medal Winner: Millennium Park, Chicago, Illinois," online at http://www.brunerfoundation.org/rba/pdfs/2009/MP.FINAL.pdf (accessed June 29, 2011).
8. Alexander, Ishikawa, and Silverstein, *Pattern Language*, 368–70.
9. Examples abound of long, narrow parks that are cherished by local residents. The 2.8-mile path around Green Lake in Seattle is by far the most heavily used part of the 324-acre park; local folklore has it that it is the most popular walking path in the United States. Almost every day thousands of people stroll, walk their dogs, or jog along the 3.5-mile Dallas Road Walkway, a band of land between Dallas Road and the Strait of Juan de Fuca in Victoria, British Columbia. Dozens of walkers (often with their dogs) can be found at all times on the Blythwood Ravine Park/Sherwood Park pathway on a narrow band of ravine land in the middle of northern Toronto.
10. Seattle Parks and Recreation, "Pro Parks Levy," last updated January 11, 2011, online at http://www.seattle.gov/parks/levy/default.htm (accessed June 29, 2011).
11. Wikipedia, s.v. "List of National Parks of the United States," last updated June 27, 2011, online at http://en.wikipedia.org/wiki/List_of_National_Parks_of_the_United_States (accessed June 29, 2011).
12. National Association of State Park Directors, "America's State Parks," online at http://www.naspd.org/ (accessed June 29, 2011).
13. Wikipedia, s.v. "List of National Parks of the United States." In the fifty years after Yellowstone National Park was established in 1872, the United States established

an additional sixteen national parks. In the next fifty years (to 1972), an additional twenty parks were set up. By 1992 fourteen more had been added, bringing the total to fifty. Since that year, eight more have been added.

14. ScienceDaily, "Attendance at U.S. State Parks Grows." A North Carolina State University study led by Dr. Yu-Fai Leung, associate professor of recreation ecology, concluded that from 2009 to 2010, America's state park attendance increased by 1.6 percent while general fund support for park operations was reduced by 12.3 percent.

15. U.S. Census Bureau, "Table 1. Urban and Rural Population, 1900 to 1990." Federal Highway Administration, "Census 2000 Population Statistics."

16. See Batker et al., "Valuing the Puget Sound Basin," 1. McClure, "Study Considers How to Make Cents of the Sound," 1.

17. Aken et al., "Transfer of Development Rights (TDR) in Washington State," 2.

8 / ON-SITE LIFE CYCLES

1. WETT, "Wastewater Treatment and Water Reclamation."

2. Natural Resources Defense Council, "Water Efficiency Saves Energy."

3. Wikipedia, s.v. "Water Supply and Sanitation in the U.S.," last updated June 25, 2011, online at http://en.wikipedia.org/wiki/Water_supply_and_sanitation_in_the_United_States#Institutional_overview (accessed July 2, 2011).

4. Stallworth, "Conservation Pricing of Water and Wastewater," 11.

5. Wikipedia, s.v. "Water Supply and Sanitation in the U.S."

6. Conference Board of Canada, "Environment: Water Consumption," October 2008, online at http://www.conferenceboard.ca/hcp/Details/Environment/water-consumption.aspx (accessed September 3, 2011).

7. Southwest Florida Water Management District, "Water Rates: Conserving Water and Protecting Revenues," online at http://www.swfwmd.state.fl.us/conservation/waterrates (accessed July 2, 2011). See also Stallworth, "Conservation Pricing of Water and Wastewater," 20.

8. Jennifer Barnes, architect and sustainability consultant, interview with Julia Levitt, April 8, 2010.

9. Fortum, "Experience and Projects," online at http://www.fortum.com/en/energy-production/combined-heat-and-power/waste-to-energy/wte-projects/pages/default.aspx (accessed June 29, 2011).

10. New Belgium Brewery, "Closing a Loop: Power from Waste Water," http://www.newbelgium.com/culture/alternatively_empowered/sustainable-business-story/planet/energy-and-greenhouse-gas-emission.aspx (accessed June 29, 2011).

11. McLennan, "Flushing Outdated Thinking," 34.

12. Clean Air Gardening, "Energy and Water Saving Shower Valve," http://www.cleanairgardening.com/shower-saver.html (accessed June 29, 2011).

13. Galbraith, "Why Is a Utility Paying Customers?"

14. State of Victoria Department of Sustainability and Environment, "Using the Integrated Water Management Provisions"; and State of Victoria Department of Human Services Environmental Health Unit, "Greywater Recycling."

9 / REGIONAL TRANSPORTATION

1. The U.S. statistics are from the Federal Highway Administration, "Census 2000 Population Statistics." The world statistics are from UN Department of Economics and Social Affairs, "World Urbanization Prospects," http://esa.un.org/unup/index .asp?panel=1 (accessed June 29, 2011). The 2007 Revision Population Database reports 2010 global population to be 6.905 billion and global urban population to be 3.496 billion, 50.6 percent of the total.

2. Cambridge Systematics Inc., *Moving Cooler,* 14.

3. Frug, *City Making,* 77.

4. Several different organizations report different percentages of households without cars for New York City, all claiming to use the 2000 U.S. Census as the source. The lowest percentage reported is 42 percent at Kathleen Maclay, "Study Explores Metro Car Ownership Patterns, Race, Segregation and Disaster Planning," *UCBerkeley News,* March 23, 2006, online at http://berkeley.edu/news/media/ releases/2006/03/23_carownership.shtml (accessed June 30, 2011). This is also the source for the 8 percent national average of households without cars. A number of other sites report percentages for New York City in the 55 percent range, including Bikes At Work Inc, "The Carefree Census Database," online at http://www .bikesatwork.com/carfree/carfree-census-database.html (accessed June 30, 2011), which reports 55.7 percent, and Wikipedia, s.v. "List of U.S. cities with most households without a car," last updated August 13, 2010, online at http://en.wikipedia.org/ wiki/List_of_U.S._cities_with_most_households_without_a_car (accessed June 30, 2011), which also reports 55.7 percent.

5. Arturo Ramos, "Major U.S. City Commute Patterns 2008," Wikimedia Commons, online at http://en.wikipedia.org/wiki/File:USCommutePatterns2006.png (accessed June 29, 2011).

6. Risa Proehl, "Certified Population Estimates for Oregon and Oregon Counties," Population Research Center, College of Urban and Public Affairs, Portland State University, December 15, 2009, online at http://www.pdx.edu/sites/www.pdx.edu .prc/files/media_assets/2009CertPopEst_web3.pdf (accessed June 30, 2011). Wikipedia, s.v. "Portland metropolitan area," last updated June 22, 2011, online at http://en.wikipedia.org/wiki/Portland_metropolitan_area (accessed June 30, 2011). The metropolitan area, including the Salem Metropolitan Statistical Area, contained 2.6 million people in 2008.

7. Wikipedia, s.v. "Transportation in Portland, Oregon," last updated May 31, 2011, online at http://en.wikipedia.org/wiki/Transportation_in_Portland,_Oregon (accessed June 30, 2011). The assertion that, at 12.6 percent of commutes, "Portland's rate of public transit use is comparable to much larger cities and higher than most similarly sized U.S. cities" is based on data from the U.S. Census Bureau, "American Community Survey 2006, Table S0802, Means of Transportation to Work by Selected Characteristics," online at http://factfinder.census.gov/servlet/ STGeoSearchByListServlet?ds_name=ACS_2008_1YR_G00_ (accessed September 5, 2011).

8. Wikipedia, s.v. "High-occupancy vehicle lane," online at http://en.wikipedia.org/wiki/High-occupancy_vehicle_lane (accessed June 30, 2011). "High Occupancy Vehicle (HOV) Systems," Virginia Department of Transportation, last updated May 20, 2011, online at http://www.vdot.virginia.gov/travel/hov-novasched.asp#I-66 (accessed June 30, 2011).

9. National Motorists Association (NMA), "NMA Position on HOV Lanes," online at http://www.motorists.org/tolls/hov-lanes (accessed June 30, 2011). The NMA says of HOV lanes: "The NMA opposes the development and designation of high-occupancy vehicle (HOV) lanes. All motorists are required to pay taxes to build the highway system, and therefore should be entitled to the full use of that system. HOV lanes depend on congestion for their appeal and thereby serve as a disincentive to reduce congestion for non-HOV lane users. HOV lanes use valuable highway corridor space that could be used to serve the entire population using that given highway, not just those who carpool or ride buses."

10. Wikipedia, s.v. "High-occupancy vehicle lane."

11. Ewing et al., *Growing Cooler,* 131.

12. Ibid., 132.

13. Ibid..

14. Ibid., 133.

15. Transportation Alternatives, "No Vacancy." This study reported that 45 percent of total traffic and 64 percent of local traffic in the Park Slope neighborhood of Brooklyn, New York, is cruising for a parking space. The study recommended the implementation of dynamic pricing for parking.

16. Adam Stein, "Bright Green: San Francisco Tests Dynamic Curbside Parking," *Worldchanging,* June 12, 2008, online at http://www.worldchanging.com/archives/008113.html (accessed June 30, 2011).

17. Wikipedia, s.v. "Congestion pricing," last updated May 13, 2011, online at http://en.wikipedia.org/wiki/Congestion_pricing (accessed June 30, 2011).

18. Oregon Department of Transportation, "Bike Bill and Use of Highway Funds," last updated February 4, 2007, online at http://www.oregon.gov/ODOT/HWY/BIKEPED/bike_bill.shtml (accessed June 30, 2011).

19. Rivera, "Bike Commuting Surges in Portland, Census Finds."

20. Ben Block, "In Amsterdam the Bicycle Still Rules," *Worldchanging,* February 20, 2009, online at http://www.worldchanging.com/archives/009450.html (accessed June 26, 2009).

21. Julia Levitt, "Underground, Automated Parking in Tokyo," *Worldchanging,* December 19, 2008, online at http://www.worldchanging.com/archives/009198.html (accessed June 26, 2011).

22. Dueker, Strathman, and Bianco, "Strategies to Attract Auto Users to Public Transportation," 41.

23. Marni Heffron of Heffron Transportation, interview with Julia Levitt, February 1, 2010.

1.   This quotation from Ford is found at http://www.goodreads.com/quotes/show/15297 (accessed June 30, 2011).

2.   Wikipedia, s.v. "History of mobile phones," online at http://en.wikipedia.org/wiki/History_of_mobile_phones (accessed June 30, 2011).

3.   Claire Bates, "Scaling New Heights: Piano Stairway Encourages Commuters to Ditch the Escalators," *Mail Online,* last updated October 12, 2009, online at http://www.dailymail.co.uk/sciencetech/article-1218944/Scaling-new-heights-Piano-stairway-encourages-commuters-ditch-escalators.html (accessed June 21, 2011). A video of the Odenplan musical stairway has become an Internet hit and can be seen at http://www.youtube.com/watch?v=2lXh2noaPyw.

4.   Wikipedia, s.v. "Farmers' Market," last updated July 1, 2011, online at http://en.wikipedia.org/wiki/Farmers'_market (accessed July 2, 2011).

5.   Mass Transit, "Beyond 'Light Rail Lite.'" The article suggests that the speed, success, and true BRT (bus rapid transit) nature of the line depends on certain characteristics being in place, including dedicated BRT lanes. The strategy of BRT has been adopted in varying formats in cities across the United States and internationally. See also Levinson et al., "Bus Rapid Transit: Volume 1," 23, which provides the following specific information about commute speeds in Bogotá: "Average speeds for BRT operations along arterial streets in the United States and Canada range from 8 to 14 miles per hour in New York City to 15 miles per hour along Wilshire Boulevard and 19 miles per hour along Ventura Boulevard in Los Angeles. 'Express' operations along Curitiba's one-way streets and Bogotá's TransMilenio busway are approximately 19 miles per hour. Buses making all stops along median busways in South America average 11 to 14 miles per hour. These speeds are low when compared with BRT operations in the United States and Canada. However, they represent dramatic improvements over local bus speeds and are often faster than automobile speeds."

6.   Wikipedia, s.v. "ARPANET," last updated June 26, 2011, online at http://en.wikipedia.org/wiki/ARPANET (accessed June 30, 2011).

7.   Walt Howe, "A Brief History of the Internet," last updated March 24, 2010, online at http://www.walthowe.com/navnet/history.html (accessed June 30, 2011).

8.   Internet World Stats, "World Internet Users and Population Stats," last updated March 31, 2011, online at http://www.internetworldstats.com/stats.htm (accessed June 30, 2011).

9.   International Internet Consortium, "Internet Domain Survey Host Count," online at http://navigators.com/stats.html (accessed June 30, 2011).

10. Internet World Stats, "World Internet Users and Population Stats."

11. Wheatley, *Leadership and the New Science*, 93.

12.   Ibid., 21.

13. Wikipedia, s.v. "Louis Pasteur," last updated August 27, 2011, online at http://en.wikipedia.org/wiki/Louis_Pasteur (accessed September 5, 2011). Wikipedia, s.v. "Timeline of immunology," last updated October 7, 2010, online at http://en.wikipedia.org/wiki/Timeline_of_immunology (accessed July 2, 2011).

14. Access Excellence, "Louis Pasteur (1822–1895)," National Health Museum, online at http://www.accessexcellence.org/RC/AB/BC/Louis_Pasteur.php (accessed July 2, 2011).

15. Wikipedia, s.v. "Life Expectancy," last updated July 2, 2011, online at http://en.wikipedia.org/wiki/Life_expectancy (accessed July 2, 2011).

16. Wheatley, *Leadership and the New Science*, 21.

17. Wikipedia, s.v. "Climate Research Unit email controversy," lasted updated August 31, 2011, online at http://en.wikipedia.org/wiki/Climatic_Research_Unit_email_controversy (accessed September 5, 2011). In November 2009 a server at the IPCC Climate Research Unit (CRU) at the University of East Anglia in the United Kingdom was hacked, which led to the release of thousands of e-mails and computer files to the Internet just a few weeks ahead of the Copenhagen Summit on climate change. Some of the scientific give-and-take in this information was exploited by climate change skeptics. Some media argued that the leaked material showed that climate scientists were systematically presenting a slanted case in favor of climate change. Most observers saw this argument as a misreading of the evidence. Six committees investigated the allegations and found no evidence of fraud or scientific misconduct.

18. City of Victoria, "Dockside Green Annual Sustainability Report 2009," online at http://www.victoria.ca/cityhall/sustainability-dockside.shtml (accessed July 1, 2011).

Bibliography

Aken, Jeff, Jeremy Eckert, Nancy Fox, and Skip Swenson. "Transfer of Development Rights (TDR) in Washington State: Overview, Benefits, and Challenges." *The Cascade Land Conservancy*. April 2008. Available online at http://ci.snohomish.wa.us/pilchuckdistrict/TDR%20Washington.pdf (accessed January 23, 2012).

Alexander, Christopher, Sara Ishikawa, and Murray Silverstein. *A Pattern Language: Towns, Buildings, Construction*. New York: Oxford University Press, 1977.

Allers, Maarten A., and Corine Hoeben. "Effects of Unit-Based Garbage Pricing: A Differences-in-Differences Approach." *Environmental Resource Economics* 45, no. 3 (September 19, 2009): 405–28. Available online at http://www.springerlink.com/content/648264643825ur07/fulltext.pdf (accessed June 25, 2011).

Ball, Jeffrey. "Six Products, Six Carbon Footprints." *Wall Street Journal*. October 6, 2008.

Batker, David, Maya Kocian, Jennifer McFadden, and Rowan Schmidt. "Valuing the Puget Sound Basin: Revealing Our Best Investments." Version 1.4, 2010. *Earth Economics*. Available online at http://www.eartheconomics.org/FileLibrary/file/Reports/Puget%20Sound%20and%20Watersheds/Puget%20Sound%20Russell/Valuing%20the%20Puget%20Sound%20Basin%20v1.0.pdf (accessed June 29, 2011).

Beatley, Timothy, and Peter Newman. *Green Urbanism Down Under*. Washington, D.C.: Island Press, 2009.

Benyus, Janine. "What Do You Mean by Biomimicry?" Biomimicry Institute. Available online at http://www.biomimicryinstitute.org/about-us/what-do-you-mean-by-the-term-biomimicry.html (accessed June 28, 2011).

Bernstein, Scott. "Testimony of Scott Bernstein, President, Center for Neighborhood Technology to the House of Representatives, Committee on Financial Services, Subcommittee on Housing and Community Opportunity." June 11, 2009. Available online at http://www".cnt.org/repository/bernstein061109.pdf (accessed June 25, 2011).

Boden, T. A., G. Marland, and R. J. Andres. *Global, Regional, and National Fossil-Fuel CO₂ Emissions.* Carbon Dioxide Information Analysis Center, Oak Ridge National Laboratory, U.S. Department of Energy. 2009. Available online at http://cdiac.ornl.gov/trends/emis/overview_2006.html (accessed June 27, 2011).

Cambridge Systematics, Inc. *Moving Cooler: An Analysis of Transportation Strategies for Reducing Carbon Emissions.* Washington, D.C.: Urban Land Institute, 2009.

Carver, Andrew D., Daniel R. Unger, and Courtney L. Parks. "Modeling Energy Savings from Urban Shade Trees: An Assessment of the CITYgreen® Energy Conservation Model." *Environmental Management* 34, no. 5 (November 2004): 650–55. Available online at http://www.springerlink.com/content/mpxk119y7kk9gp7t (accessed June 29, 2011).

Center for Neighborhood Technology (CNT). "H+T Affordability Index." Available online at http://www.htaindex.org/method.php (accessed May 30, 2011).

Darlin, Damon. "Street Corners vs. Cul de Sacs." *New York Times.* January 9, 2010. Available online at http://www.nytimes.com/2010/01/10/business/10every.html (accessed June 25, 2010).

Diamond, Rick, and Mithra Moezzi. *Changing Trends: A Brief History of the U.S. Household Consumption of Energy, Water, Food, Beverages, and Tobacco.* Lawrence Berkeley National Laboratory, undated (sources 2003 EIA data). Available online at http://epb.lbl.gov/homepages/Rick_Diamond/LBNL55011-trends.pdf (accessed June 25, 2011).

Dueker, Kenneth J., James G. Strathman, and Martha J. Bianco. "Strategies to Attract Auto Users to Public Transportation." Transportation Cooperative Research Program (TCRP) Report 40. Transportation Research Board, National Research Council. Washington, D.C.: National Academy Press, 1998. Available online at http://onlinepubs.trb.org/onlinepubs/tcrp/tcrp_rpt_40.pdf (accessed June 30, 2011).

Eckert, Vera. "World 2009 CO₂ Emissions Off by 1.3%." *Reuters News Service.* August 13, 2010. Available online at http://www.reuters.com/article/2010/08/13/us-germany-carbon-survey-idUSTRE67C1IU20100813 (accessed June 27, 2011).

Ewing, Reid, Keith Bartholomew, Steve Winkelman, Jerry Walters, and Don Chen. *Growing Cooler: The Evidence on Urban Development and Climate Change.* Washington, D.C.: Urban Land Institute, 2007.

Federal Highway Administration. "Census 2000 Population Statistics—U.S. Population Living in Urban vs. Rural Areas." Last updated May 5, 2011. Available online at http://www.fhwa.dot.gov/planning/census_issues/metropolitan_planning/cps2k.cfm (accessed June 29, 2011).

Frug, Gerald E. *City Making.* Princeton, N.J.: Princeton University Press, 1999.

Fuller, Sieglinde. "Life Cycle Cost Analysis (LCCA)." National Institute of Building Sciences, Whole Building Design Guide (WBDG). Available online at http://www.wbdg.org/resources/lcca.php (accessed June 26, 2011).

Galbraith, Kate. "Why Is a Utility Paying Customers?" *New York Times.* January 23, 2010. Available online at http://www.nytimes.com/2010/01/24/business/energy-environment/24idaho.html (accessed June 29, 2011).

Institute of Transportation Engineers (ITE). *Trip Generation, 8th Edition: An ITE Information Report.* Washington, D.C.: ITE, 2008.

Jacobs, Jane. *The Death and Life of Great American Cities*. New York: Modern Library, 1993.

Leinberger, Christopher. "The Next Slum?" *The Atlantic*. March 2008. Available online at http://www.theatlantic.com/magazine/archive/2008/03/the-next-slum/6653/ (accessed June 25, 2011).

Levinson, Herbert, Samuel Zimmerman, Jenifer Clinger, Scott Rutherford, Rodney L. Smith, John Cracknell, and Richard Soberman. "Bus Rapid Transit: Volume 1: Case Studies in Bus Rapid Transit." Transportation Cooperative Research Program (TCRP) Report 90. Transportation Research Board of the National Academies. Washington, D.C. 2003. Available online at http://onlinepubs.trb.org/onlinepubs/tcrp/tcrp_rpt_90v1.pdf (accessed June 30, 2011).

Little, Amanda. *Power Trip: From Oil Wells to Solar Cells: Our Ride to the Renewable Future.* New York: HarperCollins, 2009.

Lund, Henrik, Frede Hvelplund, Poul Alberg Østergaard, Bernd Möller, Brian Vad Mathiesen, Anders N. Anderson, Poul Erik Morthorst, Kenneth Karlsson, Peter Meibom, Mafrie Münster, Jesper Muuksgaard, Peter Karnøe, Henrik Wenzel, and Hans Henrik Lindboe. "Danish Wind Power Export and Cost." Department of Development and Planning, Aalborg University, Aalborg, Denmark. February 19, 2010. Available online at http://www.energyplanning.aau.dk/Publications/DanishWindPower.pdf (accessed July 1, 2011).

Lyttle, Bethany. "Think Small." *New York Times*. February 16, 2007. Available online at http://www.nytimes.com/2007/02/16/realestate/greathomes/16tiny.html (accessed June 25, 2011).

Marohn, Kirsti. "Habitat ReStore Outlets Growing." *USA Today*. May 18, 2011. Available online at http://www.usatoday.com/money/industries/retail/2011-05-17-habitat-humanity-restore-outlets_n.htm (accessed June 26, 2011).

Mass Transit. "Beyond 'Light Rail Lite.'" *Mass Transit*. February 25, 2011. Available online at http://www.masstransitmag.com/print/Mass-Transit/Beyond-Light-Rail-Lite/1$6162 (accessed June 30, 2011).

McClure, Robert. "Study Considers How to Make Cents of the Sound." *Seattle Post-Intelligencer*. July 24, 2008. Available online at http://www.seattlepi.com/local/372125_pugetsound25.html (accessed June 29, 2011).

McLennan, Jason. "Flushing Outdated Thinking: Transforming Our Relationship with Water." *Trimtab*. Fall 2009. Available online at http://viewer.zmags.com/publication/40152123#/40152123/34 (accessed September 10, 2011).

McNichols, Joshua. "The Rise and Fall of the Air Conditioner." *KUOW News*. May 7, 2009. Available online at http://www.kuow.org/program.php?id=17477 (accessed June 26, 2011).

Meadows, Donella. *Thinking in Systems*. White River Junction, Vt.: Chelsea Green Publishing, 2008.

Nader, Ralph, and Toby Heaps. "We Need a Global Carbon Tax." *Wall Street Journal*. December 3, 2008. Available online at http://online.wsj.com/article/SB122826696217574539.html (accessed June 25, 2011).

National Association of Home Builders (NAHB). *Housing Facts, Figures, and Trends,* March 2006. Available online at http://www.soflo.fau.edu/report/NAHBhousingfactsMarch2006.pdf (accessed June 25, 2011).

Natural Resources Defense Council. "Water Efficiency Saves Energy: Reducing Global Warming Pollution through Water Use Strategies." Available online at http://www.nrdc.org/water/files/energywater.pdf (accessed June 29, 2011).

Nowak, David J., and Daniel E. Crane. "Carbon Storage and Sequestration by Urban Trees in the USA." *Environmental Pollution* 116 (2002): 381–89. Available online at http://www.itreetools.org/eco/resources/EnvPoll_NatCarb_2002.pdf (accessed June 28, 2011).

Phillips, Michael M. "Builders Downsize the Dream Home." *Wall Street Journal*. November 13, 2009. Available online at http://online.wsj.com/article/SB125807017854346243.html (accessed June 25, 2011).

"Plane Truths: How to Build Green Planes That Airlines Will Actually Want to Fly." *The Economist*. March 10, 2011. Available online at http://www.economist.com/node/18329444 (accessed July 1, 2011).

Pryne, Eric. "Modern Rooming House Offers Cable-Ready, Furnished Rooms—The Size of a Parking Spot." *Seattle Times*. July 23, 2009. Available online at http://seattletimes.nwsource.com/html/localnews/2009520937_roominghouse23.html (accessed June 26, 2011).

Public Policy Institute of California. "Special Survey on Californians and Their Housing." *PPIC Statewide Survey*. November 2004. Available online at http://www.ppic.org/content/pubs/survey/S_1104MBS.pdf (accessed June 25, 2011).

Rivera, Dylan. "Bike Commuting Surges in Portland, Census Finds." *The Oregonian*. September 23, 2009. Available online at http://www.oregonlive.com/news/index.ssf/2009/09/bike_commuting_surges_in_portl.html (accessed June 30, 2011).

Rosenthal, Elisabeth. "In German Suburb, Life Goes On without Cars." *New York Times*. May 11, 2009. Available online at http://www.nytimes.com/2009/05/12/science/earth/12suburb.html?_r=2 (accessed June 27, 2011).

ScienceDaily. "Attendance at U.S. State Parks Grows, Even as Funding Decreases." *ScienceDaily*. March 16, 2011. Available online at http://www.sciencedaily.com/releases/2011/03/110316153125.htm (accessed June 29, 2011).

Sharman, Hugh. "Why Wind Power Works in Denmark." In *Proceedings of ICE, Civil Engineering*. London: Thomas Telford, Ltd., 2005. Available online at http://www.incoteco.com/upload/CIEN.158.2.66.pdf (accessed September 10, 2011).

Smith, Adam. *An Inquiry into the Nature and Causes of the Wealth of Nations*. Edited by Edwin Cannan. 5th ed. London: Methuen and Co., Ltd., 1904.

Stallworth, Holly. "Conservation Pricing of Water and Wastewater." April 10, 2000. Available online at http://www.epa.gov/OW-OWM.html/cwfinance/cwsrf/consrvprice.pdf (accessed July 2, 2011).

State of Victoria Department of Human Services Environmental Health Unit. "Greywater Recycling: Appropriate Uses." Available online at http://www.health.vic.gov.au/environment/downloads/greywater_usage.pdf (accessed June 29, 2011).

State of Victoria Department of Sustainability and Environment. "Using the Integrated Water Management Provisions of Clause 56, Residential Subdivision." October 2006. Available online at http://www.dpcd.vic.gov.au/__data/assets/pdf_file/0020/41717/VPP_Clause_56_4-Intwaterman.pdf (accessed June 29, 2011).

Stern, Nicholas. *The Global Deal: Climate Change and the Creation of a New Era of Progress and Prosperity*. London: The Bodley Head, 2009.

Taylor, Rob, and Jonathan Standing. "Drought in Australia Food Bowl Continues." *Reuters News Service*. February 3, 2009. Available online at http://www.reuters.com/article/ idUSTRE5127CY20090203 (accessed May 30, 2011).

Transportation Alternatives. "No Vacancy: Park Slope's Parking Problem and How to Fix It." February 2007. Available online at http://www.transalt.org/files/newsroom/reports/ novacancy.pdf (accessed June 30, 2011).

United Nations Department of Economics and Social Affairs. "World Urbanization Prospects." Available online at http://esa.un.org/unup/index.asp?panel=1 (accessed June 29, 2011).

U.S. Census Bureau. "Table 1. Urban and Rural Population, 1900 to 1990." Released October 1995. Available online at http://www.census.gov/population/censusdata/urpop0090.txt (accessed June 29, 2011).

U.S. Department of Transportation Office of Public Affairs. "DOT Secretary Ray LaHood, HUD Secretary Shaun Donovan, and EPA Administrator Lisa Jackson Announce Interagency Partnership for Sustainable Communities." June 16, 2009. Available online at http://www.dot.gov/affairs/2009/dot8009.htm (accessed June 28, 2011).

U.S. Energy Information Administration. "Annual Energy Review 2009." Report No. DOE/ EIA-0384(2009). August 19, 2010. Available online at http://www.eia.doe.gov/emeu/ aer/elect.html (accessed June 25, 2011).

———. "Share of Energy by Appliances and Consumer Electronics Increases in U.S. Homes." Residential Energy Consumption Survey (RECS). March 28, 2011. Available online at http://www.eia.gov/consumption/residential/reports/electronics.cfm (accessed June 25, 2011).

U.S. Environmental Protection Agency. "Cap and Trade: Acid Rain Program Basics." Undated. Available online at http://www.epa.gov/captrade/documents/arbasics.pdf (accessed June 25, 2011).

U.S. Green Building Council. "What LEED Is." Available online at http://www.usgbc.org/ DisplayPage.aspx?CMSPageID=1988 (accessed June 27, 2011).

WETT (Water Energy Technology Team). "Wastewater Treatment and Water Reclamation." Lawrence Berkeley National Laboratory. Undated. Available online at http://water-energy.lbl.gov/node/16 (accessed June 29, 2011).

Wheatley, Margaret J. *Leadership and the New Science: Discovering Order in a Chaotic World*. 3d ed. San Francisco, Calif.: Berrett-Koehler, 2006.

Wilson, Jonathan B., Maura A. Marcheski, and Elias B. Hinckley. "The Great PACE Controversy: Renewable Energy Financing Program Hits a Snag." *Probate and Property* 25, no. 3 (May–June 2011). Available online at http://www.kilpatricktownsend.com/~/media/ Files/articles/2011/Wilsonv25n3.ashx (accessed June 27, 2011).

Index

Boeing, 27–28

Bogotá, Colombia, 124, 139–40, 167n5

Boston, 82

Brookings Institution, 22–23, 135

BRT (bus rapid transit), 139–40, 167n5

building codes: affordable, compact housing and, 58–59; building types, discrepancies in, 75; as impediments, 9; on-site life cycles and, 113; TDM and, 132. *See also* regulation; zoning

buildings, commercial: "cold, dark shell," 62; energy disclosure, 59–60; evolution of office systems, 69; hotels, LEED standards for, 22; life-cycle cost analysis on owner-occupied and build-to-suit buildings, 61–62; obsolete, 65; office space per worker, 54; passive cooling, 62, 160n22; separate metering by tenant, 62–63. *See also* developers; on-site life cycles for water and energy; reuse, restoration, and retrofits

buildings, residential. *See* housing and residential buildings

businesses, private-sector: bicycle commuting, building-level support for, 134; coalitions and, 50–52; defined, 156n7; frameworks adjustments by, 39–40; parking, unbundling from rental rates, 130–32; private shuttles, complementary, 132–34; regulatory feedback from, 49–50; reuse and, 76–78; standards generation and measurement systems and, 21–23; telecommuting and, 134

bus lanes, 124

bus rapid transit (BRT), 139–40, 167n5

C

Canada: College Street area, Toronto, 82; Dockside Green, Victoria, 145–46; Gooderham and Worts Distillery, Toronto, 66, 67f, 68; tax rebates, 35; water systems, 107

cap and trade, 32–33, 36

carbon, embodied, 76, 126

carbon dioxide (CO_2) emissions: carbon fixation by greenspaces, 95–96; carbon tax correlated with, 36, 37f; educational institutions and, 23; international emissions targets and scaling problem, 18–19; life-cycle impact, 17–18, 17t; measurement of, 13–15, 14f; as steady state, 4–5; sulfur dioxide (SO_2) emissions vs., 32–33; targets and target setting, 18–20. *See also specific topics*

carbon efficiency, defined, 9

carbon footprint, reducing. *See specific topics*

carbon sinks, 100

carbon tax: in British Columbia, 33; federal imposition of, 29–33; market disadvantage, avoiding, 37; objections, and keeping net tax revenue constant, 33–36; regulatory alignment and, 44–45; road capacity and, 123; at source, 36, 37f; transition cost and, 38–39

Cascade Land Conservancy. *See* Forterra

Cash for Clunkers program, 43

cell phones, 26, 137, 138f

Center for Neighborhood Technology (CNT), 22–23, 56–57

Center for Transit Oriented Development (CTOD), 22–23

change. *See* innovation, change, and delight

chaos and innovation, 10–11

Chicago, 96–97

children, 97–98, 103–4

city governments. *See* local governments

City Making (Frug), 119–20

Cityscape Holdings, 66

Citytank.org, 93

climate change. *See specific topics*

clothing reuse or retrofit, 66

cloud computing, 148

Cluny–La Sorbonne station, Paris Metro, 138

CNT (Center for Neighborhood Technology), 22–23, 56–57

coalitions and collaboration, 50–52

College Street area, Toronto, 82
Colombia, 124, 139–40, 167n5
commercial buildings. *See* buildings, commercial
commodities trading, 15–16
compact development: "good density" vs. "bad density," 82–83; historical preservation and, 74; infill development projects, 48, 84–85; rural preservation and, 99; state legislative barriers to, 43, 85; system boundaries and, 48, 85–86; upzoning and alternatives, 89–90; zoning and, 58. *See also* neighborhoods, compact and complete; zoning
composting, 108
Conference of Mayors Climate Protection Center, U.S., 31
congestion pricing, 127–28
Congress, U.S., 32
Container City (London), 66–68, 67f
cooling, passive, 62
cottage housing developments (Seattle), 59
Craigslist, 69
crime, perception of, 6
CTOD (Center for Transit Oriented Development), 22–23
currency markets, 26
cycling, 128–30, 130f, 134

D

Daley, Richard M., 96–97
data vs. anecdotes, 6
deconstruction, 68, 74
delight. *See* innovation, change, and delight
demand-pricing for parking, 127
Denmark, 45–46
density. *See* compact development; neighborhoods, compact and complete
design for reuse, 68–70. *See also* reuse, restoration, and retrofits
developers: contaminated infill sites, liability protection for cleanup of, 72–73; defined, 156n7; energy efficiency vs.

affordability and, 35; framework adjustments and, 39–40; innovation, role in, 147–50; life-cycle cost analysis on owner-occupied and build-to-suit buildings, 61–62; metering, separate, 62–63; on-site life cycle technology and, 116; parking, unbundling from rental rates, 130–32; reuse and, 68, 76–78; semi-private or shared open spaces, 103–4; streamlined permitting for deconstruction, 74
discounted cash flow model, 78
disposal, design for, 68
distributed generation, regulation for, 45–46
Dockside Green, Victoria, BC, 145–46
doughnut approach to zoning, 89–90
Drucker, Peter, 13

E

Earth Economics, 100–101
economic frameworks. *See* frameworks
Economist, The, 26
eco village developments, 92
educational institutions: energy retrofits, 23–24, 76–77; Internet development at, 140; regional transportation system cost models from, 134–35; testing and feedback on standards by, 23–24
efficiency: carbon tax and, 36; off-site life cycles and inefficiencies, 106–8; road capacity allocated by person-trip efficiency, 124–25; trip bundling and lost time, 121
Einstein, Albert, 136
EISs. *See* environmental impact statement (EIS) analysis
electrical outlets, standardization of, 26
electricity: generation capacity, maximization of, 42–43; off-site life cycles and inefficiencies, 107–8; sources of, 36, 37f; transmission power losses, 46, 159n6; from waste incineration in Stockholm, 109. *See also* energy

Institute of Transportation Engineers (ITE), 47–48
institutions, 8, 9, 155n7
interagency partnerships, 23
Intergovernmental Panel on Climate Change (IPCC), 144, 168n17
international emissions targets, 18–19
international markets, 37, 80–81
international treaties, 31–32
Internet and World Wide Web, development of, 140–42, 141f
Internet service providers (ISPs), 112
investors, 116, 147–50, 156n7
invisible hand, 26
IPCC (Intergovernmental Panel on Climate Change), 144, 168n17
Ishikawa, Sara, 97–98
ISO standards, 21
ITE (Institute of Transportation Engineers), 47–48

J

Japan, 95
Jones Lang LaSalle, 60
Joseph Vance Building, Seattle, 67f

K

King County, WA. See Seattle and Puget Sound
Kirkland, WA, 48–49

L

landfill sites, exchange facilities at, 73
Last Chance Mercantile (Monterey, CA), 73
laws, and framework failure, 8. See also regulation
Leadership and the New Science (Wheatley), 142–43
LEED (Leadership in Energy and Environmental Design): Dockside Green, Victoria, BC, and, 145–46; for existing buildings (LEED-EB), 76; floor-area ratio and, in Seattle, 42; hotels and, 22; King County, WA, and, 16–17; Living Building Challenge, 111; for Neighborhood Development, 111; new construction (NC) program, 76; operational and per capita considerations in, 59; Weber Thompson headquarters, Seattle, 62
Leinberger, Christopher, 135
lending. *See* financing, funding, and lending
LessEn (Urban Land Institute), 60
level of service (LOS) models, 86–87
leverage points (Meadows), 5
liability management, 72–73, 115
LIDs (local improvement districts), 114
life-cycle analyses, 17–18, 17t, 77–78, 126. *See also* on-site life cycles for water and energy
Living Building Challenge, 111
local governments: frameworks adjustments by, 39; game theory problem and, 31; measurement systems and, 20; neighborhoods and, 88–93; on-site life cycles and, 113–15; parks and nature in cities, 101–2; "reduce" and, 58–59; reuse and, 73–75; system boundaries for EISs, redefining, 47–48; transportation networks and, 126–30; water and electricity pricing, 34–35. *See also* transportation networks, regional; zoning
local improvement districts (LIDs), 114
location-efficient mortgages, 56–57
London, 66–68, 67f, 127–28
Los Altos Hill, CA, 74
LOS (level of service) models, 86–87
low-income citizens, 35

M

maintenance, design for, 68
manufacturing vs. service economy, 65
Marcheski, Maura, 72
marginal cost basis, 46–47
McKinstry, 133–34

Meadows, Donella, 5

measurement systems: adopting the leading system (federal), 18–19; CO2 emissions and, 13–15, 14f; definition of, 13; examples of, 15–18; feedback about regional subgoals, 20; frameworks and, 25; generation of standards by nonprofits and businesses, 21–22; imperfect models and, 15; national and regional target-setting and PDCA, 19–20, 20t; promotion and interagency partnerships, 22–23; state and local adoption of national standards, 20; strategy, 18; testing and feedback from educational and research institutions, 23–24

media, 6, 146–47, 168n17

methane, 109

metric system, 15

metropolitan planning organizations (MPOs), 126

metro stations, 138

microhomes, 54–55

Microsoft, 54, 133

milk packaging, 55–56, 55f

mixed-use development and zoning regulation, 43, 88–89. *See also* neighborhoods, compact and complete

mobility: increasing, 120–21; level of service and, 87; neighborhoods and, 79–81; transportation funding and, 125–26. *See also* transit; transportation networks, regional

models: imperfect, 15, 16; level of service (LOS), 86–87; regional transportation system cost models, 134–35; transformative innovation and, 28

Monterey Regional Waste Management District (CA), 73

mortgages, location-efficient, 56–57

mother-in-law apartments, 90

Mother Teresa, 64

MPOs (metropolitan planning organizations), 126

Muir, John, 94

N

National Motorists Association (NMA), 124, 166n9

National Strategy on Energy Efficiency (Australia), 59

National Trust for Historic Preservation, 75

nature and green spaces: appreciation for and contact with, 94–95; benefits from, 95–97; incorporating nature into cities, 101–2; local parks, 101; national and state forests as carbon sinks, 100–101; national and state parks, 99–100; needs and wants for, 97–99; neighborhoods and green space requirements, 91; nonprofits as advocates for, 103; roof decks, 91; semiprivate or shared open spaces, 103–4; strategy, 99; transfer of development rights (TDRs), 99, 102

neighborhoods, compact and complete: Dockside Green, Victoria, BC, 145–46; examples of, 81–82; global market and, 80–81; "good" vs. "bad" density, 82–83; HUD funding for, 83–84; importance of, 79–80; level of service (LOS) models and, 86–87; mixed-use zoning and, 88–89; nonprofits and, 93; on-site life cycles compared to, 105–6; parking requirements and, 90–91; reuse and, 68; single-family developments, sustainable, 91–93; state barriers to, 84–85; strategy, 83; system boundaries, revising for, 85–86; upzoning and auxiliary housing, 89–90; and urban public schools, 88; vehicle miles traveled (VMT) emissions credits, 87–88

Netherlands, 34, 65, 129, 158n11

New Belgium Brewing Company (Fort Collins, CO), 109

New Building Institute, 75

New Construction (NC) program, 76

"New View of the Puget Sound Economy, A" (Earth Economics), 100–101

R

rail systems. *See* transit

Realty Check events (Urban Land Institute), 50–51

recreational spaces. *See* nature and green spaces

recycling, 42, 64–65. *See also* reuse, restoration, and retrofits

reducing: agriculture subsidies and, 57; garbage, 34, 158n11; home size trends and, 53–54; life-cycle cost analysis on owner-occupied and build-to-suit buildings, 61–62; location-efficient mortgages, 56–57; market transparency in energy use and, 59–60; microhomes, 54–55; milk packaging, 55–56, 55f; office space per worker, 54; operational and per capita considerations in certification, 59; separate metering for tenants and, 62–63; strategy, 56; zoning and building codes for affordable and compact housing, 58–59

Reed, Bill, 94–95

regional governments. *See* local governments

regulation: alignment, meaning of, 41–42; carbon tax and subsidy, 44–45; coalitions and collaboration and, 50–52; examples of barriers and alignment, 42–44; framework failure and, 8; laws and framework failure, 8; marginal cost vs. average cost for energy, 46–47; nonprofits and business, role of, 49–50; on-site life cycles and, 115; state-regional-local balance for environmental protection policies, 48–49; strategy, 44; and system boundaries for EISs, 47–48; underlying agency problem, 11; utilities, aligning for conservation and distributed generation, 45–46. *See also* environmental impact statement (EIS) analysis; federal government; state governments; zoning; *specific agencies*

renewable energy credits, 113

research institutions, 23–24, 140

residential buildings. *See* housing and residential buildings

resilience in systems theory, 4

restoration. *See* reuse, restoration, and retrofits

The ReStore (Habitat for Humanity), 69

retrofits. *See* reuse, restoration, and retrofits

reuse, restoration, and retrofits: building codes and building types discrepancies, 75; and contaminated-site clean up, 72–73; deconstruction, streamlined permitting for, 74; definitions, 64; design for reuse, 68–70; embodied-carbon transparency, 76; energy retrofit loans, 77; energy retrofits at educational institutions, 23–24, 76–77; examples of, 66–68, 67f; exchange facilities for building material reuse, 73; and historical preservation, 74–75; HUD funding and long-term, high-quality housing, 70–71; LEED and Living Building Challenge and, 76; life-cycle costing, 77–78; PACE financing for energy retrofits, 71–72; quality and, 66; recycling vs. reuse, 64–65; service economy and, 65; strategy, 70

reverse metering, 45–46

rights, human, 34

Riknäs, Mikhael, 157n3(ch2)

roads. *See* transportation networks, regional

roof decks, 91

Rose Smart Growth Investment Fund, 66

S

salvaged building parts, market for, 73

San Francisco, 127

schools, urban, 88

Seattle and Puget Sound (city and region): Children's Hospital and SEPA, 49; cottage housing developments, 59; energy codes and, 75; Growing Transit Communities (Puget Sound Regional Coun-

Victoria, Australia, 115
Victoria, British Columbia, 145–46
visionaries, 152
vision for climate stability, 8–9
VMT (vehicle miles traveled), 87–88, 125
Volkswagen, 138
voluntary carbon reduction, game theory
    problem in, 31

W

walking paths, 98, 101
Walk Score, 87
Wall Street Journal, 17, 24
Washington State: Department of Ecology
    and LEED and piecemeal incentives,
    42; energy disclosure for nonresidential
    buildings, 59–60; Growth Management
    Act, 43; state park campsites, 100. *See
    also* Seattle and Puget Sound
Washington State Environmental Policy Act
    (SEPA), 16–17, 43, 49, 85, 86
waste and wastewater management. *See* on-
    site life cycles for water and energy
waste incineration in Stockholm, 109
water, potable, grey, and black, 109–10
water pricing, 29–31, 33, 37–38
water systems. *See* on-site life cycles for
    water and energy
Weber Thompson, 62
Wheatley, Margaret, 142–43, 144
Wilder, Laura Ingalls, 80
Wilson, Jonathan, 72
wind power, 45–46, 148

Z

zoning: for affordable and compact housing,
    58–59; cottage housing developments
    and (Seattle), 59; mixed-use develop-
    ment and, 43, 88–89; on-site life cycles
    and, 114–15; for semiprivate or shared
    open spaces, 103–4; TDR policies, 102;
    upzoning and alternatives, 89–90. *See
    also* building codes